RELATIVISM, NIHILISM, AND GOD

Library of Religious Philosophy

Thomas V. Morris, editor

Volume 2

RELATIVISM, NIHILISM, AND GOD

PHILIP E. DEVINE

University of Notre Dame Press
Notre Dame, Indiana

Copyright © 1989 by
University of Notre Dame Press
Notre Dame, Indiana 46556
All Rights Reserved
Manufactured in the United States of America

The author gratefully acknowledges permission to reprint in revised form portions of this work which he has had published as journal articles.

"The Public Responsibilities of Philosophers" first appeared in *Teaching Philosophy* published by The Philosophy Documentation Center.

"Relativism" first appeared in *The Monist*. Copyright © 1984, *The Monist*, LaSalle, Illinois 61301. Reprinted with permission.

An earlier version of chapter 6 appeared as "Theism: An Epistemological Defense" in *The Thomist* 50 (1986): 210-222.

Part of chapter 7 is reprinted from *Faith and Philosophy*, Vol. 3, no. 3 (July, 1986), pp. 270-284 by permission of the editors.

Library of Congress Cataloging-in-Publication Data

Devine, Philip E., 1944–
  Relativism, nihilism, and God /
Philip E. Devine.
    p. cm.—(Library of religious philosophy; 2)
  Bibliography: p.
  ISBN 0-268-01640-2
  1. Pragmatism. 2. Relativity. 3. Nihilism.
4. God. 5. Theism.
6. Religion. I. Title. II. Series.
B832.D48   1989
144'.3—dc20
                                                    89-40387

Ab uno te adversus in multis evanui.
[I turned away from the one You and
wasted myself on the many.]
St. Augustine

CONTENTS

PREFACE · xi

1. INTRODUCTION · 1
   The Aim of This Book, 1
   Terminological Issues, 3
   An Example: Psychical Research, 6

2. THE PUBLIC RESPONSIBILITIES · 11
   OF PHILOSOPHERS
   Philosophy and Propaganda, 12
   What Are Philosophers For?, 16
   Some Implications, 18
   Concluding Remarks, 20

3. PRAGMATISM · 23
   The Ambiguities of Pragmatism, 23
   First Interpretation: A Relativism of Multiple Ends, 28
   Second Interpretation: Might as Right, 30
   Third Interpretation: The Sovereignty of the Good, 33

4. RELATIVISM · 37
   The Concept of a Framework, 37
   Further Preliminaries, 41
   The Relativist Argument, 42
   Relativism Assessed, 46

5. NIHILISM — 57
   Varieties of Nihilism, 57
   Deconstruction, Politics, and Sex, 62
   The Death of God, 69
   Repressing Nihilism, 72
   Accepting Nihilism, 74
   Transcending Nihilism, 75

6. GOD — 77
   The Moral Argument, 77
   The Argument Continued, 79
   Morality and Rationality, 82
   Is It God?, 84

7. RELIGION — 93
   On Defining *Religion*, 93
   Religion Defined, 95
   Religious Truth, 101
   Conclusion, 109

   NOTES — 111

LIBRARY OF RELIGIOUS PHILOSOPHY

The Library of Religious Philosophy has been established to encourage and make available philosophically well informed essays on a variety of central religious topics, as well as religiously sensitive and theologically motivated treatments of traditional philosophical issues. Priority will be given to books written in a lively and broadly accessible style, which focus on subjects of great general interest, as over against highly formalized and technically narrow treatises on topics mainly of interest just to specialists in the field.

It is our goal to stimulate the publication of books characterized as much by genuine philosophical insight, and even a spirit of wisdom, as by technical rigor and clarity of expression. It is anticipated that volumes in the Library will broach such topics as the nature of God, the shape of a meaningful human existence, the idea of salvation, life after death, the contours of a philosophically responsible religious world-view, and the reasonableness of religious faith, and well as many of the other perennial questions of philosophy.

Thomas V. Morris
General Editor

PREFACE

THIS BOOK IS A DEFENSE of the reality of God in the sense in which Nietzsche proclaimed His death. On the way to this defense, I set forth and critically examine three views that, in one way or another, accept the death of God and take it as central to the intellectual life: *pragmatism*, which takes as the only end of the intellectual life the furtherance of this-worldly goods other than Truth; *relativism*, which admits a multiplicity of truths corresponding to the multitude of modes of life pursued by human beings; and *nihilism*, according to which the pursuit of Truth is a sham. I then set out and defend my own position and connect it with the religious doctrines to which it is indebted and lends some support, but with which it is not to be confused.

A persistent source of confusion—invited by the word *absolutism*—is the idea that relativism means moral laxity, or even the view that all moral rules have exceptions (however rare). Whether there are exceptionless moral rules is an important and interesting question, but it is not the question addressed in this book.

The arguments of this book presuppose the rejection of two common fallacies: the strict fact/value distinction, and the confusion of relativism and tolerance. For present purposes, it is sufficient to state dogmatically that the fact/value distinction is one of degree only. All our cognition is laden with purpose and evaluation: objectivity itself is a moral and (as in

Spinoza) a spiritual ideal. Hence, for example, there is no value-neutral language available in which to discuss difficult human problems.

I have elsewhere criticized those who would use relativism to advance the cause of tolerance (*Philosophy and Phenomenological Research* 48 [1987]: 131–38). Very briefly, if there are no common standards to which disputants can appeal, a struggle to the death is as likely a result as is tolerance. At best, one can expect those practicing diverse modes of life to define and defend—and from time to time to struggle over—their turf.

I here argue for a convergence between the concerns of philosophy and those of faith. I therefore open myself to the charge of equivocating between religious and philosophical conceptions of Truth, and of illegitimately attempting to exploit the advantages of both. In order to address this charge, I examine the view that can be summed up in the phrase "Philosophy for the few, religion for the many." For short, I shall call this the *elitist view*.

We may distinguish three aspects of the elitist view. At its crudest, it maintains that religious beliefs, though false, are nonetheless necessary to support the social order. More subtly, a philosopher who himself rejects religion can nonetheless respect the religion of others insofar as it makes it possible for them to enjoy goods that they might not otherwise realize. For many people the alternative to religious faith is not philosophical wisdom, but a life devoted entirely to the satisfaction of appetite and ambition. Finally, the elitist view can acknowledge that Christianity, for example, contains important truths, which philosophy is in the process of translating into conceptually adequate terms. To avoid arrogance the elitist philosopher had best not claim to understand Christianity completely: he cannot avoid issuing a promissory note on the future of philosophical inquiry.

At this point the elitist tradition encounters an important divide. Some elitists—Marx perhaps—regard the division between the many and the few as a temporary and remediable feature of the human situation. In any plausible version this branch of the elitist view supposes deep political and social transformation, as well as mass education, before the many are capable of philosophical wisdom. For another sort of elitist—Leo Strauss perhaps—the division between the many and the few is a permanent feature of human life.

One objection to the elitist view is that Christianity—or more exactly Christian orthodoxy—is true and requires no translation into more adequate concepts. But this objection begs the question: even if it is granted that a system of religion is true, by the criteria appropriate to religious truth, the issue of the nature of religious truth remains. The elitist asserts that religion has, at best, a second-rate sort of truth, suitable for the many but not for the enlightened few.

A second objection is a democratic protest against the division between the many and the few that the elitist view proposes. To this the elitist will retort that the division between the many and the few is a fact, however much those of democratic sympathies may regret it. In its more attractive forms, elitism will counsel respectful silence in the face of the errors of religion, except when one is teaching one's chosen disciples, and support for religious institutions based on a sense of their utility. This support can be given in a way that does not imply acceptance of the truth of religious beliefs; as George Washington attended Episcopal services without taking Communion. And the elitist will regard acquiescence in religious error as a temporary expedient, to be used until the many attain a level of enlightenment compatible with philosophical wisdom.

A third and more potent objection is that the elitist view overstates the gap between philosophers and other persons: philosophers, like ordinary folk, experience the crises that require a religious response; philosophers, like ordinary folk, die. Hence for a philosopher, as for anyone, the landscape of one's imagination is an important concern. To this objection a defender of elitism will respond that the philosopher (or other unbelieving intellectual) can obtain the required intellectual sustenance from culture (in Matthew Arnold's, not the anthropological, sense).

I now introduce a technical term. By *amplitude* I mean that feature of an expression of culture (a poem, for example) that enables an unbeliever to use it to meet the needs that believers satisfy with the help of their faith. By an easy extension, a situation can be said to possess amplitude just in case it calls forth amplitude of expression. Although I have introduced the concept of amplitude to illumine the problems of unbelieving intellectuals, its scope is wide enough to include traditional religious language as well. Hence the protests that have been registered, in the name of culture, against the shelving of the King James Bible, the Latin Mass, and the Book of Common Prayer.

Any situation, if experienced by a sufficiently sensitive person, can possess amplitude. But some situations call for amplitude from nearly everyone, to the extent that the absence of such a response is evidence of diminished humanity. Chief among these is death, whether one's own death in prospect or the death of a friend as an event in one's own life. Others are sexual experience (at least where it has emotional importance), maturation, acknowledgment of guilt, marriage, birth and rearing of children, and in general all those transitions that affect a person's understanding of himself. To these may be added the corresponding events in the life of a community, such as the transmission and transformation of political authority.

An analogy may help the reader understand what I mean by amplitude and the argumentative use I make of it. What is called strong language—that employed by human beings to express violent hostility or frustration—falls into three classes: the religious, the sexual, and the excretory. That the profane use of religious language is dependent upon its primary use requires no argument. And even sexual and excretory profanity carries with it an implicit metaphysics: it consigns its objects to a condition dominated by physiological processes and needs, while presuming that such a condition involves an important loss.

Let me not be misunderstood. "Fuck you," "Eat shit," and

"Go to hell" have negligible amplitude, unless a skillful writer manages to supply them with a transforming context. My argument runs as follows: if profane language has metaphysical or religious implications, how much more so must language possessing the required amplitude.

The dilemma of the unbelieving philosopher is therefore as follows. He requires amplitude of expression to deal with the experiences he shares with other human beings. Yet his unbelief isolates him from at least one source of amplitude. And the culture to which he turns contains many elements that, implicitly at least, appeal to transcendent religious notions. How then can he enjoy the benefit of amplitude without paying the price of belief?

At this point the argument branches. One branch makes no claim to rigor but, if successful, will persuade the reader that something like traditional religion is required. The other, though more rigorous, has a weaker conclusion.

The forms of expression to which poets and others turn for amplitude are indebted to traditional religion, even when the poet himself is an avowed atheist. And appropriate language cannot be created at will, but must be nurtured across a number of generations. Even imagining a source of amplitude other than religion of a recognizably traditional sort encounters serious obstacles.

There are, to be sure, various religion surrogates (or untraditional religions) to which an unbelieving poet might turn in his search for amplitude. But these are either limited in their scope (as is liberalism), merely negative (as is anticommunism), or dependent for their energy upon residues of traditional religion (as is Marxism). Those who turn to such religion surrogates in their search for amplitude are therefore likely to find them inadequate. The great religions are precisely those that have nourished the imaginations of many generations.

The second branch of the argument is a priori. It asks wherein consists the amplitude that an unbeliever might seek from culture, being unable to get it directly from religion. The answer is that language has amplitude when it can persuade us that the requirements of our emotions and imagination have metaphysical warrant. In the face of the death of a friend, for example, we need to be persuaded that we were entitled to value him as we did and that what we valued in him will not be wholly lost, in the face of what appears to be the contrary verdict of nature. In the search for amplitude appropriate to grief, as in weddings-and-funerals religion, there is some tolerance for suspended disbelief. But this tolerance is not without limit. And to speak of metaphysical support for the demands of our emotions and imagination—or, from the other side, of emotion and imagination informed by metaphysics—is to speak of religion, though not necessarily of religion of a recognizably traditional sort.

The argument so far has not been a defense of some specific form of religion. Many forms of religion are capable of meeting its requirements. Which a person embraces will depend on a number of further considerations. But one criterion that sharply limits the systems of religion a person might consider is that it should be possible, within an acceptable religion, not only to satisfy the requirements of imagination and emotion but also to preserve and develop one's intellectual powers.

A view of religion that I find more sympathetic than elitism can be summed up as follows: God (or the Divine) is infinitely mysterious: we should therefore worship Him (or Her or Them or It) as is most expedient, usually, though not invariably, in accordance with the conventions of our group. In some cases this may mean not worshipping at all. In dealing with this view, I shall set to one side the claims of revelation to qualify the mystery of the Divine and to set limits to the modes of worship (and other behavior) open to human beings.

Now the question immediately arises, What does *expedient* mean in this context? We have no right to suppose that, whereas the concept of religious truth is opaque, that of helping us cope is transparent and easy to apply. If, like Pascal, we wager on our state hereafter, the terms of the wager will be affected by the very mystery we are trying to circumvent. The calculus of chances is ill-suited to deal with infinite goods and infinite evils. But if expedience is measured wholly in this-worldly terms, then our religion will be reduced to some blend of politics and therapy.

And, whatever the brand of politics or therapy one embraces, this kind of reductionist religion quickly loses credibility. Men and women of faith should identify themselves with those this-worldly forces that, in the light of their faith, they regard as tending to bring about the good life for human beings. But if their religion is only an auxiliary to worldly causes, it can always be outbid by those who pursue such causes without religiously motivated inhibitions. The appeal of religious beliefs and practices rests crucially on their ability at least to gesture toward a perspective transcending the conflicts that permeate human social life. Hence, for example, the integrity of religious symbols must be preserved even when that preservation is the source of conflict with forces in one's society that one is reluctant to offend.

Yet there are some virtues in religious pragmatism. What these are can be best seen by a consideration of some attitudes called "fundamentalist" when they occur in Protestants and "integralist" when they occur in Roman Catholics. An Anglican convert to Catholicism manifests such an attitude when he remarks, of the doctrine of papal infallibility, "The Church has the bomb" (Sheldon Vanauken, "The English Channel," *The New Catholics*, ed. Dan O'Neill [New York: Crossroads, 1987], 129).

It is easy to sympathize with the demand for an authority capable of putting to rout all the confusions of the modern era, whether one finds that authority in the infallibility of the Pope or the verbal inerrancy of Scripture. But the demand for an escape from modernity is to be resisted nonetheless, just as much as the attempt to resolve the tension between Christianity and the modern world by reducing Christian faith to a political or therapeutic ideology.

For the demand for a "bomb" leads to treating one's faith, by implication at least, as a fantasy world into which one can retreat, or a perch from which one can look down on others, rather than a resource on which one can draw in one's life and the life of one's society. Modernity is neither a virtue nor a plague, but simply a fact: this side of Jordan, the modern world is the only one in which we are able to live.

Hence what is needed is a religion that makes possible a stance of critical empathy and empathetic criticism of contemporary culture. The next question is, What doctrine of spiritual authority is most appropriate in the light of this requirement? My inclination is to say that what we need is an intellectual, moral, and spiritual community that at the same time credibly portrays itself as the vehicle of God's presence in the world and accepts without reservation the fact that it is a human institution subject to all the deficiencies of such institutions. (Such a community would, among other things, provide a sound basis for political action.) In such a community claims to absolute authority would not be renounced altogether; neither would they be easily or quickly made. Whether and how this conception could be embodied in the present world seem to be genuinely open questions.

Two points of usage need attention. Although not desiring to give offense to anyone, I find that the custom of writing "he or she" destroys my writing style, and the common gender "she" merely creates confusion. Accordingly "he" is here used in the common gender sense except when the context requires a male individual. I also use a capital "He" for the deity: this is to be read as a special pronoun designed for such use, which does not beg the question of God's gender.

Chapters 1, 3, and 5 of the present book are entirely new. The remaining chapters have been published as follows: chapter 2 in *Teaching Philosophy* 10 (1987): 3–12; chapter 4 in the *Monist* 67 (1984): 405–18; chapter 6 in the *Thomist* 50 (1986): 210–22; and chapter 7 in *Faith and Philosophy* 3 (1986): 270–84. Each article has been carefully revised for inclusion in this book. I have also given lectures based on this book at Stonehill College and at Saint Socrates Society, Boston College.

The present book is the product of more than fifteen years as a gypsy scholar: I did work on it at Rensselaer Polytechnic Institute; the University of Wisconsin, La Crosse; the University of Scranton; Saint Cloud State University; Stonehill College (whose excellent computer system was of particular value); the University without Walls, University of Massachusetts; Lesley College; and Tufts University. Summer work at Brown University; Wellesley College; the University of Nebraska, Lincoln; the University of Notre Dame; and Tufts University was of particular importance. And most of all a year's study at the Harvard Law School brought home to me the necessity of addressing the problems of this book and of upholding the existence of Truth against those who see only a struggle for power.

In the course of writing, I have acquired more debts than I am able to discharge. I wish, however, to thank the following, dialogue with whom was in one way or another crucial: Myron Anderson, Leonard Champney, Peter Garber, Ronald Glass, Duncan Kennedy, Roger Guttentag, James Goldfarb Devine, David Jacobosky, James Nelson, Robert Rafalko, Joseph Ryshpan, Patrick Walker, James Woodward, and above all Celia Wolf-Devine. Tom Morris's editorial comments forced me to clarify some crucial issues. Thanks also are due to Celia and to Patrick for their help in proofreading this manuscript, and to Father Lockary for setting me up on Stonehill's computer.

1

INTRODUCTION

IN ORDER TO SET THE scene for the more developed arguments of this book, I begin by attempting three preliminary tasks: outlining the aim of the book, laying down some crucial terminology, and illustrating my central themes with the help of the example of psychical research. The discussion of psychical phenomena will be particularly concerned to show that the problems addressed in this book have a practical importance, one that extends to questions of fact as well as those of value.

THE AIM OF THIS BOOK

"There is one thing a professor can be certain of," Allan Bloom has recently written, "almost every student entering the university believes, or says he believes, that truth is relative."[1] And Bloom provides the following illustration of his thesis: "If I pose routine questions designed to confute them and make them think, such as 'If you had been a British administrator in India, would you have let the natives under your governance burn the widow at the funeral of a man who died?' they either remain silent or reply that the British should never have been there in the first place."

Any teacher can confirm the accuracy of Bloom's observation: what may be called *student relativism* is endemic in our universities. And any philosopher can confirm the further observation that such relativism is not merely a given fact, but is reinforced by many "educators," especially in the social sciences.

Student relativism is easily refuted. For it asserts two incompatible propositions: first, that all modes of life are of equal value, and second that some modes of life—those characterized by "tolerance" and "openness"—are to be preferred to others. And the student relativist cannot coherently reject modes of life founded on claims to truth transcending human purposes and conventions, yet he is required by the logic of his position to reject such claims.

More sophisticated variations on student relativism can be refuted almost as easily. A social scientist dismisses all appeals to truth or justice as ideological mystifications. Yet he argues as if justice requires him, and us, to further the interests of groups of which he, and we, are not members: those not belonging to one of the privileged oppressed groups are consigned to a position of permanent inferiority. Were he the spokesman of some group of which he was a member, or that had engaged his services for pay, his position would be at least intelligible; as things stand, it remains opaque.

A legal scholar or literary critic holds that a text can be made to mean whatever the reader pleases: the outcome of "the struggle for the text" is determined by power relations alone.[2] Hence the United States Constitution can be read as a charter for hereditary monarchy, the *Communist Manifesto* as mystical theology, and *Humanae Vitae* as authorizing sexual license. Such positions are thoroughly nihilistic in their implications: if a writing or speech can be made to mean anything one pleases, then a sentence appearing to assert a proposition can be made to assert its negation. Hence there is no difference between truth and error, and hence no possibility of reasoned assertion, or of assertion as opposed to the expression of emotion.

One need only apply such positions to deconstructionists such as Derrida or Foucault in order to refute them. One can read Derrida or Foucault as arguing that the Pope must be supreme in both spiritual and temporal matters and find no principled grounds to resist such an interpretation. Nor can they, consistent with their commitments, assert that their views on language are true. Yet I am guided as I write by the conviction that, although we should in the end reject relativism, there is a great deal more to it than someone like Bloom supposes.

My aim in this book is twofold. First, I inquire whether relativism and its allies can be reformulated in such a way as to prevent immediately devastating objections. My strategy will be to distinguish two levels, at the first of which it is possible to make ordinary truth claims, and at the second of which relativism and allied philosophies can be pursued. Second, I investigate what is required for an adequate refutation of relativism and its allies: very briefly, I maintain that we require belief in the reality of God in the sense in which Nietzsche proclaimed His death.

In the remainder of this chapter, I set up a usable terminology and employ the example of psychical research to illustrate the problems to be addressed in this book. The chapters that follow proceed as follows. I begin by articulating a traditional conception of the task of philosophy, in response to the recent revival of interest in applied or special ethics. I then consider three progressively more extreme ways of rejecting this conception—pragmatism, relativism, and nihilism. I then respond to these philosophies by formulating an epistemological defense of theism. Finally, I consider religion, that is, those imaginative representations that provide the links between the universal cognitive and evaluative standpoint attributed to God and the necessarily limited perspectives of human beings.

TERMINOLOGICAL ISSUES

Central to the argument of this book is a distinction between two levels of discourse. The first or *experiential* level consists in statements made on ordinary occasions, be they scientific, commonsense empirical, ethical, religious, or aesthetic. Examples of statements at the experiential level are as follows:

1. $E = mc^2$
2. Brockton is south of Boston.
3. It is wrong to lie to congressional investigators about covert operations.
4. God has the power to deliver us from the power of evil.
5. Michelangelo's *David* is a great work of art.

The second or *critical* (also called *criterial*)[3] level involves statements employed in the assessment of statements at the experiential level. Examples of statements at the critical level are as follows:

6. An acceptable scientific hypothesis must be testable in repeatable experiments.
7. Nature is regular.
8. Actions are to be judged by their effects on human happiness.
9. Popes and general councils are infallible on questions of faith and morals.
10. Unity is a virtue in works of art.

What I have in mind can be briefly developed as follows. Human beings, just by virtue of their existence in the world, hold and express beliefs; as Hume saw, man is a believing being. But the experience of error—and of disagreement with those with whom we have to live—leads to the formulations designed to resolve doubts and settle controversy. When these latter formulations are in doubt, we have the beginnings of an epistemological crisis, whereas doubts at the first level are the ordinary stuff of human intellectual and social life.

The distinction just made between the experiential and the critical levels is subject to four qualifications. First, the distinction is context-relative: a statement that is experiential in one context may be criterial in another, and *vice versa*. It might seem that expressions of the form "It appears to me that" (or "I think that") are a special case. (Such expressions can be followed by any statement, including those listed as [1] through [10] here.) But even such statements are experiential when they are part of the speaker's autobiography (their criteria of truth are the same as those of their sincerity), and criterial when coherence with appearance is taken as a standard of truth.

Second, there may be, under appropriate circumstances, not two but many levels of discourse, so that intermediate levels are criterial with respect to those below them and experiential with respect to those above them. The laws of science are usually criterial for the statements made in engineering; they are usually experiential with respect to those made in the philosophy of science.

Third, the selection of statements to employ as criterial depends on one's intended audience. In discussions among Christians, the existence of God can be taken for granted; not so in discussions between Christians and naturalists.

Fourth, there are philosophical views that imply a rejection of the criterial/experiential distinction. These include a naive realism, according to which there can be an unmediated encounter between the mind and its objects, so that all of our knowledge can be experiential in character; and a thoroughgoing epistemological nihilism, which reduces all discourse to the response of an organism to its environment, to which critical questions are irrelevant.

But the views to be considered in this book all take for granted the reality of the criterial/experiential distinction. All leave the experiential level as it is, at least provisionally, but assert contrasting positions about the criterial level.

11. *Nihilism* holds that from a critical standpoint all statements made at the experiential level are unwarranted.
12. *Pragmatism* holds that the criterion by which statements at the experiential level are to be judged is that of their utility (or else that the criteria by which we judge our experiential statements are to be assessed in terms of their utility).

13. *Relativism* holds that there is an irreducible multiplicity of incompatible critical criteria, above which no further criterion can be found.
14. *Platonism* holds that there is truth at the criterial level, in as good a sense as at the experiential level.
15. A special form of Platonism is *theism*, which envisages this truth as the judgments of an all-wise Judge.

Distinguishing the criterial and the experiential levels also makes it necessary to distinguish among senses of *truth*. I use *truth* with a small *t* as a general word of assent, neutral among the various views to be examined in this book; something like the disquotational theory of truth is appropriate for it. *Truth* with a capital *T* means truth in the fully Platonic sense: in other words, believers in Truth reject any version of the claim that truth is what my peers will let me get away with or that truth is what advances the cause of revolution. Finally *correctness* or *orthodoxy* (as a non-Christian can speak of orthodox Christianity or a non-Marxist of orthodox Marxism) will mean truth within a stipulated framework, concerning whose status no questions are asked. This conception of truth will be of particular interest to those attracted to relativism.

AN EXAMPLE: PSYCHICAL RESEARCH

The crucial presupposition at stake in psychical research has been well formulated by C. E. Hansel: "ESP can only be possible if there are new, at present unknown, processes and properties of matter that permit it to take place."[4] Those who accept this presupposition will evaluate the evidence for parapsychology differently than those who reject it.

I provisionally assume that the evidence for the existence of parapsychological phenomena is strong enough that the results cannot be dismissed as resulting from chance alone.[5] And if one accepts such results at face value, they require major modifications in existing scientific paradigms. Hence there are strong a priori pressures to explain away such results.

For some writers—usually called "skeptics," although their skepticism is very narrowly directed—such pressures are for all practical purposes absolute. One such writer cites Lucian:

> To defend one's mind against these follies, a man must have an adamantine faith, so that even if he is not able to detect the precise trick, by which the illusion is produced, he at any rate retains his conviction that the whole thing is a lie and an impossibility.

And more bluntly Tom Paine: "Is it more probable that nature should go out of her course, or that a man should lie?"[6] For such a writer, a controlled experiment is one whose controls are sufficient to extinguish the supposed effect.

Among the strategies used to explain away parapsychological phenomena, the charge of fraud has a special role. For if an experimental result arises through conscious fraud, then there is nothing further to discuss. (In contrast, unconscious fraud and "sensory leakage" raise complex issues about unconscious mental processes.) And controls for fraud can never be complete: an experimenter could always lie about his experiment; a skeptical witness could always be suborned. And fraud has been detected in every branch of experimental science, including parapsychology.

Moreover, charges of fraud raise sensitive questions of experimental method that may take psychical phenomena outside the realm of science altogether. If the demand for control is rejected on the ground that the mere presence of a skeptical inquirer is sufficient to destroy an effect, then the suspicion of fraudulence is difficult to dispel. Furthermore, even an eyewitness may suspect that he is dealing with a miracle, rather than a repeatable event within the compass of the natural sciences (or secular history).[7] The appropriate critical principles for dealing with supposed miracles are those of theology, including the important principle that not all spirits are of God.

Yet controls for fraud encounter a problem that is endemic to psychological research and that is especially acute if the causal connections supposed by parapsychology exist. The attitudes of the experimenter, and the fact of experimentation itself, are known to affect the data. And if psychic powers, in fact, exist, the experimental subject will be able to detect a hostile attitude by other than normal sensory means. Hence the appropriate tightness of control is a central issue for psychical research. Even if one does not set up an experiment with the unexpressed purpose of destroying parapsychological effects, it is not methodologically innocent to require psychical researchers, and not researchers in educational psychology, to defeat a presumption of fraudulence.

Another resource for the skeptic is to withdraw the concession cited at the outset of this discussion, and to hold that what are apparently the results of psychic powers arise from chance. This proposal also raises an a priori issue: what are the appropriate antecedent probabilities? For just as any experimental result can be ascribed to fraud, any experimental result can be ascribed to chance. The point at which the invocation of chance strains credulity depends on one's understanding of the sort of world in which one lives.

A final a priori issue is related to the role of the natural sciences as cultural guardians. For science in our world is not merely an investigation of natural phenomena and a source of technologically valuable information but also an authority by appeal to which pseudosciences such as astrology are rejected. A guardian of scientific orthodoxy can ply his trade without being exposed to the kind of hostility Cardinal Ratzinger has encountered. But the simple scientific worldview associated with Newtonian mechanics is now in very bad repair: as a result many scientists and friends of science fear that if parapsychology is admitted to the ranks of legitimate sciences, no barriers to credulity will remain.

If the argument of this section is sound, both critics and proponents of parapsychology must attend to the a priori issues. Both must make explicit and defend the standards of experimental credibility they employ, and defenders of parapsychology must produce coherent theories in which their experimental procedures make sense. Producing and debunking experimental results will otherwise have extremely limited persuasive effects. And for present purposes the most important implication is the centrality of the issues to be discussed in this book. For differences at the criterial level can have enormous importance at the experiential level, even when the question at issue is one of fact, such as whether psychical phenomena in fact occur.

In sum: this book is concerned with formulating and criticizing relativism and a family of related antirealist doctrines. In this chapter I have been concerned with laying out the central concepts around which my argument will turn and with illustrating the crucial distinction between the criterial and the experiential levels of discourse.

2

THE PUBLIC RESPONSIBILITIES
OF PHILOSOPHERS

ONE OF THE MORE REMARKABLE features of the recent history of philosophy is the explosion of interest in questions of public philosophy and what is somewhat unfortunately called "applied ethics."[1] A profession whose members not so long ago were deeply worried about the possibility of providing rational support for even the simplest, least controversial moral judgments has thrown itself with enthusiasm into the complexities of concrete moral and political issues. The fruits of this development have included not only books, articles, courses, fellowships, and other conventional manifestations of the academic life but also testimony before a presidential commission, interviews on television and radio, and even a congressional campaign or two.[2]

The author has taken part in this movement,[3] but now considers it desirable to reflect critically on it. Engagement with practical issues quickly discloses clashes of worldview, and these clashes pose the issue of relativism that is a central concern of this book. The traditional philosophical task, of finding a Truth transcending human purposes and conventions, conflicts deeply with the partisan spirit that informs most discussion of concrete issues. The problems raised by Machiavelli arise not only in the sphere of action but in that of the intellect as well.

The applied philosophy movement has served the excellent purposes of gaining economic support for philosophers and their families and of subsidizing more conventional philosophical enterprises. But if it serves only these purposes, the discussion of applied ethics will fail even to support philosophy and philosophers. Philosophers must convince both themselves and others that they have a distinctive contribution to make to the public debate, even to sustain their contribution to that debate as a source of material reward.

Three interlocking questions can be distinguished. First, what does a philosopher have to contribute to the public debate about such issues as nuclear deterrence? Second, what is gained, from a philosophical point of view, by attempting to apply philosophical theories and concepts to contested public issues? Third, when a philosopher examines such an issue, in what relation does he stand to those whose concern is at best secondarily with Truth? We must specially deal with the charge that by purporting to stand aside from the conflicts of the day and take a position of independent judgment, the philosopher is abandoning the field to those whose triumph will guarantee the destruction of everything the philosopher is protecting.[4]

PHILOSOPHY AND PROPAGANDA

We may distinguish three arguments whose intent is to show that philosophers should renounce their distinctive concerns and devote their efforts to propaganda. One of these may be called the argument from inevitability, the second the civic responsibility argument, the third the Chicken Little argument.

The argument from inevitability maintains that philosophers, like it or not, are advocates of a certain point of view. A value-free, detached perspective on the universe, or on the problems of philosophy, is impossible. A pretense of having taken such a point of view serves no ends except those of mystification.

It is of course the case that Plato, Spinoza, and Kant are advocates of certain points of view. But that does not make them propagandists. A propagandist—more politely a publicist—writes to a brief external to his argument: writes to a brief supplied by a source outside his argument; a philosopher is at liberty to develop his point of view and the arguments for it together. By this standard, the only major philosopher who can be accused with any plausibility of being a propagandist is St. Thomas Aquinas. But even this charge would be unfair. What is distinctive about St. Thomas is not his Catholicism, but his attempt to correlate the teachings of the Church with the findings of reason and specifically with the philosophy of Aristotle. This project was controversial when St. Thomas wrote, and, despite a period of enforced Thomism, remains so among Catholics today.[5]

The civic responsibility argument points out that philosophers do not cease to be citizens. As such they have the same duties as other citizens, which may range according to circumstance from voting to participation in revolution. As intelligent persons, they have the duty to discern and expose sham and to make known the truth as they see it in the public forum.

Yet not everything a philosopher does he does as a philosopher. Despite Plato, what a philosopher says to his beloved in an erotic situation may have very little philosophical about it. Likewise a philosopher who makes a political speech need not do so philosophically: it is an open question whether he can do so without injury to both his philosophy and his politics.

The Chicken Little argument points to the dangerous state of the world and urges that the philosopher abandon his academic scruples and devote every effort to the prevention of disaster. The threat of nuclear annihilation provides the most plausible example here; it does not matter much, if at all, whether we conceive the threat as to the continued existence of the human race or "only" to civilization. But it is a feature of the politics of our time that there is virtually no issue that cannot be presented in apocalyptic terms. It follows that, if we await a world that is not in serious danger to undertake philosophy, we will have to postpone philosophical inquiry indefinitely. Hence philosophers should examine the Chicken Little argument with particular care.

If it could be established that by abandoning their academic preoccupations, and only by so doing, philosophers could prevent nuclear annihilation, it would be our duty to do so. In the absence of any evidence of such power of philosophers, however, we should examine more closely the philosophical issues the Chicken Little argument raises.

One is how we know the sky is falling. Even a remote possibility of thermonuclear annihilation should be a matter of the most serious concern, but evidence of the degree of danger is open to interpretation. And once the need to interpret evidence is admitted, a wide range of philosophical questions becomes relevant.

It is also necessary to ask why the sky is falling. If systematic habits of deceit constitute even a part of the reason for our peril,[6] then it is at best maladroit to counsel philosophers to abandon their traditional concern for intellectual integrity. At least we require some way of deciding which lies are most likely to preserve the human enterprise.

Again, we must ask what measures, if any, are likely to prevent the sky from falling, or to limit the damage if it falls. To be committed to the prevention of nuclear holocaust is not the same thing as to embrace any particular strategy for avoiding it, or even to exclude advocacy of civil defense in case our efforts fail. Issues of strategy and tactics should be debated on their merits and cannot be settled by declaring the urgency of preventing nuclear war. And to make a contribution to these debates will require more of philosophers than adherence to a certain party.

The most radical question is why we should care whether the sky falls. If human civilization survives as long as I expect to live, then mere self-preservation will not motivate me to go to its defense. And there are many people who seem quite prepared to risk nuclear conflagration in the hope that it will at least destroy their enemies.[7] More radically, someone disgusted with civilized life might prefer its destruction to its continuance, even if its destruction should be attended by immense suffering. The value of human life, and the activities and experiences characteristic of it, requires defense or at least critical discussion. And the same is true of the value of continued civilization.

Some or all of these issues might be neglected as a result of the urgencies of political action. But it is one thing to respond to these urgencies and another to destroy the discipline that addresses questions postponed in political action by demanding that it subordinate itself to a political program. Even the view that questions of evidence and value require no further answer than is needed for practice is a philosophical position requiring a philosophical defense.

Those who ask philosophers to become propagandists may hold that everyone should be a propagandist—that not just philosophy but all forms of human activity should be subordinated to the urgencies of political action. The connection between such an attitude and some of the worst developments in twentieth-century history is strong enough to make this position distinctly unattractive.

The most fundamental requirement of propaganda is the study of the passions of the human beast. To enlist the aid of philosophers in a propaganda war is to suppose that among these passions is an instinct for Truth, for which philosophers are required to provide at least the appearance of satisfaction. Philosophers, and scholars of every sort, are required to provide the footnotes by which an appeal to passion can be disguised as a result of critical inquiry. Once again, we must ask whether the perilous state of the world is even partly the result of systematic habits of deceit; and, if so, what possibly could lead us to believe that what is needed, by way of an attempt to remedy this situation, is the introduction of yet another element of deceit.

But if philosophers do not make suitable propagandists, then the question arises what the proper role of philosophy is, if indeed philosophy has any proper role at all.

WHAT ARE PHILOSOPHERS FOR?

It is sometimes complained, of the *Apology of Socrates*, that it falls short of Plato's usual standard of intellectual honesty, in that only Socrates' side of the issue is presented. But a careful reading will not only allow us to discover the case made by Socrates' accusers but show that their complaint and Socrates' defense are very much the same. As frequently happens in cases of ideological conflict, the reasons Socrates advances in his own defense are very similar to those that motivate his accusers and judges to bring about his death.

A philosopher can state the case against philosophy more effectively than can its avowed opponents. The shared ideas that make human cooperation possible are a public good, comparable to a system of currency. Like counterfeiting, a threat to the stability of these ideas, though it sheds no visible blood, threatens every member of society. And philosophical reflection, however conservative its conclusions, tends to undermine belief in these ideas and to provide excuses by which members of society can justify their departure from its rules. Only unthinking conformity, the enemies of philosophy argue, can prevent the dissolution of society into a multitude of warring factions.

Mill's arguments for tolerating actions harmful only to consenting parties are irrelevant here: the charge against philosophy is that it threatens every member of society by damaging those institutions on which he relies for his well-being. And sermons against conformity are also irrelevant, unless one is prepared to accept social chaos in the desperate hope that something of value may emerge from it. The case for freedom of thought, and for the liberal freedoms generally, must therefore rest not on the harmlessness of their exercise but on the benefits to be derived from them.

No one these days proposes to forbid philosophy by law, and even the attempt to prevent philosophers from reaching unpopular conclusions is relatively unimportant. But this does not mean that the issues raised by the *Apology* are now limited in their relevance to advocacy in the narrow sense. To make my point, I need only cite the rueful remark of a philosopher friend of mine, that he would stop trying to get his students to think until he had tenure. The crucial issue for a contemporary discussion of the value of philosophy is in a word economic.

We must therefore address the question, What about philosophy requires, not just the tolerance, but the support of society? Our answer will have implications for the further question, What kinds of philosophy most deserve support? And the answer to both questions will have to be linked to the motives that keep a philosopher going, despite the sordidness of academic politics and the many other obstacles that stand in the way of his work.

Some of the arguments for philosophy, and for the liberal arts generally, stress their usefulness for a variety of external ends. The ability to present abstract ideas clearly is of value in a number of fields from computer science to law. The reasoned discussion of moral and political issues may further social peace and thus indirectly even economic productivity.

But vocational and political arguments like these suffer from the same deficiencies as attempts to win support for the arts by arguing that playgoers patronize hotdog stands. In the absence of arguments showing that philosophy advances such goals more effectively than do other disciplines, they are at best indecisive. And philosophers should be wary of arguments that, in their professional capacity of promoters of reasoned argument, they would indignantly reject. Socrates would have scorned a proposal that he measure his success by his usefulness to the political and economic elite.

The vocational concerns of contemporary students are understandable, but sometimes at least they must take second place to the need of society to educate its citizens and potential leaders. And this requires, among other things, that we educate the rising generation in the tradition of controversial moral and political issues. When a philosophy teacher addresses the issue of abortion or Zionism, for example, his conclusions may not be as important as his attempt to convey to students the fact that such issues are capable of reasoned discussion. A supposedly educated population that is ignorant of the tradition of reasoned ethical discourse is an appalling prospect. Not just shared evaluations and other beliefs, but a tradition of critical examination and sometimes revision of these evaluations is a public good in the contemporary world.

But anyone who takes applied ethics seriously will quickly discover the inadequacy of the fragmentary and ad hoc treatments of persistent philosophical issues that a concentration on applied ethics alone entails. For that reason, no philosophy department will be content to be a department of applied ethics. And no course or article on applied ethics will be remotely adequate unless it contains a discussion of the issues of metaphysics and ethical theory that it raises. Merely to conjoin an ethical theory with a problem—say to apply Rawls to sexual morality or to the question of nuclear power—is to produce absurd and unconvincing results.

And philosophy is not only useful to this or that end but good in itself. Nor are these two arguments for philosophy in any tension with one another. Like friendship, philosophical reflection is both an end and a means: in Cardinal Newman's words, it is both good and productive of good.

SOME IMPLICATIONS

It is now time to draw some conclusions concerning the disputes of philosophers about the way their enterprise should be conducted. Richard Rorty has recently argued that philosophers should abandon their search for a Truth transcending human purposes and conventions and content themselves with interpreting the forms of discourse produced by human beings. His argument will have to be considered in detail. But for now it is sufficient to notice that it raises the delicate question of whether society should be asked to support the self-liquidation of philosophy or whether it would not make better sense to transfer to other fields the funds that would otherwise go to a field one of whose leaders has apparently proposed its dissolution.[8] The issue cannot be settled within the philosophical community itself (for philosophers are interested parties), nor can it be resolved by asking where the truth lies. For Rorty insists that he and his "Platonist" opponents lack a shared conception of truth in whose terms their dispute could be settled.

The issue between Rorty and the tradition needs to be addressed on pragmatic grounds, for want of any better. Those philosophers who believe in a Truth transcending human purposes and conventions will more effectively maintain dialogue among rival modes of thought than those who believe that such rivalries represent only the divergent responses of human organisms to their environments. And there are strong pragmatic reasons not to try to live in the twentieth century without the belief famously formulated by George Orwell: that there is truth, and there is untruth, and that those who cling to the truth, even against the whole world, are not mad.

Second, we must expect a continuing tension between a philosopher's interest in argument and the interest he shares with other human beings in the conclusions of his argument. Though a philosopher is not a publicist, his conclusions will place him in alliance with some publicists, and the groups they represent, and in opposition to others.

Although it is not the business of a philosopher to produce bad arguments for good causes, he may occasionally feel reluctant to criticize the bad arguments of his allies. Yet, since a bad argument for a true conclusion may contain within itself the seeds of serious error, a philosopher must also pay heed to the teaching of the *Gorgias* that the proper use of the art of words is to accuse oneself and one's friends (480 c–d). Especially to be avoided is the suppression of considerations that might "play into the hands of the enemy."

The most distinctive public responsibility is not tied to any particular issue. It is to do what we can to produce citizens who are aware of the issues and the tradition of discussing them rationally. This principle entails two different principles governing our professional lives: first, that we must maintain the link between teaching and scholarship, so that the pursuit of Truth can be meshed with the need to make contributions to the public dialogue; second, that we must resist, so far as the requirements of survival permit, pressures to coddle students or to define teaching effectiveness in terms of popularity. The critical examination of cherished beliefs is often a painful process—though it can also be a source of deep pleasure—and demanding that those who induce it be always popular is profoundly destructive of the educational enterprise.

CONCLUDING REMARKS

"It is the responsibility of intellectuals," Noam Chomsky has written, "to speak the truth and expose lies."[9] This formulation suffers from two deficiencies. First, especially where instrumentalist conceptions of truth are influential, the distinction between truth and useful lies tends to lose focus, particularly as we become aware of the diversity of the criteria by which human beings judge contested issues. Second, once the distinction between Truth and party interest has been admitted, it is absurd to suppose that Truth or lies will be found exclusively on one side of a dispute. Against Chomsky in particular, it is worth pointing out that not everything a spokesman for the American elite says is a lie.

To reject a partisan conception of truth is not to adopt an imaginary value-free perspective. Nor is to become a "hired gun" for some party other than Chomsky's. It is rather to defend a central commitment of philosophers from Socrates on. That the involvement of intellectuals in politics should raise the issue of the nature of truth is as good a justification of the traditional concerns of philosophers, and in particular those explored in this book, as can be expected. And it is both the central responsibility of philosophers and their most distinctive contribution to the public debate to preserve, in precept and example, the distinction between Truth and what serves the interest of some party. And this remains the case, however modest a given philosopher's claim to personal possession of such Truth may be.

So far I have set out a traditional conception of the role of philosophy. But it is now necessary to consider three positions that increasingly repudiate such a role for philosophy. They are pragmatism, relativism, and nihilism.

3

PRAGMATISM

AGAINST THE CONCEPTION OF philosophy outlined in the last chapter stands the pragmatic tradition of James, Dewey, and Rorty. But what pragmatism is exactly is not at once clear.

THE AMBIGUITIES OF PRAGMATISM

Pragmatism has at least two distinguishable senses. The more traditional sense is a definition or criterion of truth: truth is what "works" or "fits."[1] The clearest (and bluntest) formulation of this position is that of William James: "The true... is only the expedient in our way of thinking."[2]

But Richard Rorty has developed a possibly different sense of pragmatism:

> A pragmatic theory about truth says that truth is not the sort of thing one should expect to have a philosophically interesting theory about. For pragmatism, "truth" is just the name of a property which all true statements share. (xiii)[3]

So far the distinctive character of pragmatism may seem to have been lost. All that we apparently have here is an entirely reasonable decision to do without a definition of truth, pragmatic or other.

But Rorty develops his account further by citing the "battle between... the gods and the giants" (xv)—between adherents of a transcendent criterion of truth and those for whom the primary sense of "truth" is empirical. For Rorty, pragmatism cuts across the distinction between transcendent and empirical conceptions of truth by rejecting the presupposition, common to both parties, that there is an invidious distinction between kinds of truths.

Thus the pragmatist shares with the positivist the notion that knowledge is power. But he carries this notion through to its logical conclusion; the positivist does not. He therefore altogether drops the notion of truth (at least in any sense involving correspondence with reality). Rather than saying that modern science enables us to cope because it corresponds with reality, Rorty limits himself to saying that enables us to cope (xvi–xviii).

And no one who follows Rorty with respect to science can resist a similar approach to other sorts of discourse. A consistent pragmatist would not ask whether the statements characteristic of a religion or of a political ideology are true (in any sense that invites comparison with external reality): he would ask instead whether they help their adherents cope, for example by maintaining solidarity within a group and assisting them in retaining or obtaining a position of power or in protecting one another in a position of weakness. The same question can be asked for an individual: the value of his ideas to him will have to be judged by the extent to which they help him cope: in the case of an academic, truth will be what gets him tenure.

From this characterization of questions of truth, Rorty draws some conclusions about how philosophy is to be conducted.[4] Both analytic and Continental philosophy, he argues, have been moving in a pragmatist direction, a direction he wishes to encourage.

> James and Dewey were not only waiting at the end of the dialectical road which analytic philosophy travelled, but are waiting at the end of the road which, for example, Foucault and Deleuze are currently travelling. (xviii)

For example: Rorty sees Dewey and Foucault as presenting complementary pictures of the social sciences. Dewey emphasizes their role in widening and deepening our sense of community and of the possibilities open to this community, whereas Foucault emphasizes their use as instruments of social discipline (204). But both are to be praised for their attempt

> to free mankind from Nietzsche's "longest lie," the notion that outside the haphazard and perilous experiments we perform there lies something (God, Science, Rationality, or Truth) which will, if only we perform the correct rituals, step in to save us. (208)[5]

Rorty ends his discussion of Dewey and Foucault by remarking that Dewey is to be preferred to Foucault, on the ground that his vocabulary allows room for an unjustifiable hope and for a groundless but vital sense of human solidarity (208).

One cannot help but ask on what grounds Rorty holds that the "longest lie" is in fact a lie (there are people who believe it) or what grounds he might have for evaluating Dewey and Foucault as he does. It is hard to see how what he says in this connection would make the least impression on a person who regarded human solidarity as an illusion and struggle for power as the only reality of human life.

Rorty goes on to urge the development of a "post-Philosophical culture," one that refuses "to accept the Philosophical distinction between first-rate truth-by-correspondence and second-rate truth-as-what-is-good-to-believe" (xxxvii). Such a culture will be one in which

> neither the priests nor the physicists nor the poets nor the Party [are] thought of as more "rational" or more "scientific" or "deeper" than one another.... There [will] be no sense that beyond the current intra-disciplinary criteria which, for example, good priests and good physicists obeyed, there were other, transdisciplinary, transcultural, ahistorical criteria which they also obeyed. (xxxviii)

It would also contain nobody called "the Philosopher" who could explain why and how certain areas of culture enjoyed a special relation to reality, though it would contain "all-purpose intellectuals" who would be ready to offer a view on pretty much everything, in the hope of making it hang together with everything else (xxxix). Rorty expects cracker-barrel intellectuals of this sort to take the place of academic philosophers.

Rorty acknowledges that his views imply that

> when the secret police come, when the torturers violate the innocent, there is nothing to be said to them of the form "There is something within you that you are betraying. Though you embody the practices of a totalitarian society which will endure forever, there is something beyond these practices which condemns you.". . . There is nothing deep down inside us that we have not created in the course of creating a practice, no standard of rationality that is not an appeal to such a criterion, no rigorous argument that is not obedience to our own conventions. (xlii)

Rorty describes the movement from Platonism or positivism to pragmatism as the progress toward doing without God. This means not only the rejection of Biblical religion and all its easily recognizable descendants; it also means the rejection of the positivist attempt to establish Science as an idol to fill the place once held by God (xliii).

The crucial question is "whether a post-Philosophical culture is a good thing to try for" (xliii). On this issue Rorty concludes:

> There is no way in which the issue between the pragmatist and his opponent can be tightened up and resolved according to criteria agreed to by both sides. This is one of those issues that puts everything up for grabs at once—where there is no point in trying to find agreement with "the data" or agreement about what would count as settling the question. But the messiness of the issue is not a reason for setting it aside. The issue between religion and secularism was no less messy, but it was important that it got settled as it did. (xliii).[6]

The issue, he says, "will be decided, if history allows us the leisure to decide such issues, only by a slow and painful choice between alternative self-images" (xliv). The movement from Platonism and positivism to pragmatism has, in other words, many of the attributes of a leap of faith.

The exposition so far raises six questions for pragmatism:

1. At what level does pragmatism operate? Does it apply directly to statements at the experiential level, or does it apply rather to the criteria according to which such statements are judged?
2. Does pragmatism involve the invocation of a criterion, or is it a form of epistemic nihilism, for which statements are nothing more than the responses of organisms to their environment?
3. If pragmatism does involve the invocation of a criterion, what is the relationship between that criterion and the more mundane criteria employed by scientists and others in their work?
4. Supposing that pragmatism involves judging beliefs by their contribution to some end:
   a. What is the end that beliefs are supposed to promote? Is it pleasure, survival, eternal blessedness, or something else?
   b. How does one assess the proposition that a belief promotes an end? Does not the assertion that a belief promotes an end have to be nonpragmatically true?
5. How does the pragmatist respond to the argument that pragmatism refutes itself, that there are excellent pragmatic reasons for being, say, a Platonist?
6. A pragmatist cannot assert that his Platonist opponent is wrong, since he lacks the relevant concept of wrongness. Cannot the Platonist ignore the pragmatist or at least respond to his arguments with the words of Kafka: "God will cheat no one, not even the world of its triumph?"

In the remainder of this chapter I consider three interpretations of pragmatism, with special emphasis on the answer each of them gives to these six questions.

FIRST INTERPRETATION: A RELATIVISM OF MULTIPLE ENDS

The simplest version of pragmatism is frankly relativistic. Ideas are assessed in accordance with their ability to further the purposes of some individual or group. These ends are taken as givens: no question about whether they are worthy of pursuit is admissible. The concept of truth is then either redefined accordingly or else replaced by some other concept such as correctness. The instrumentalist criterion here suggested is applied directly to beliefs, without the intervention of any other criterion. Let us call this interpretation of pragmatism *simple instrumentalism*.

Simple instrumentalism has both individualistic and collectivistic variants. Henry VIII desired Anne Boleyn and legitimate issue; it suited these purposes for him to believe— and get others to believe—that his marriage to Catherine of Aragon was invalid and that the Pope had no legitimate power in England. It suits the organizational ends of a defense contractor for its employees to believe—and persuade others—that the hostility between the United States and the Soviet Union is irreconcilable. Individuals and groups having different ends will reach different conclusions when their beliefs are determined in this way.

Although the simple instrumentalist purports to remain neutral among ends, there is at least one end he cannot countenance: pursuit of Truth. The author once put the following question to a disciple of Rorty: does not the story of Socrates have pragmatic value, in that it helps believers in Truth cope? And he received the inevitable answer, that since there is no such thing as Truth, it would be unfortunate that the story of Socrates should be given such a use. How this end alone can be ruled out of court is by no means clear.

Moreover, the simple instrumentalist faces two problems when he considers more ordinary criteria of truth. First, even simple instrumentalists will not usually invoke only instrumentalist arguments when they try to persuade themselves and others to accept instrumentally useful positions. Hence revealing the instrumentalistic basis of a person's beliefs is perceived as unmasking, and the movement from instrumentalistic to noninstrumentalistic criteria as donning of a mask.

Second, the instrumentalist requires a noninstrumentalist conception of truth to validate the premise that a certain belief will help us achieve our ends. If the question of whether a certain belief will have the desired effect arises, the answer cannot be given in terms of the effects of belief, for that would lead to an infinite regress.

The only way an instrumentalist can escape these problems is to abandon the notion that instrumentalism involves the application of a criterion. Instead, those largely unconscious processes by which a human being adapts to his environment replace criteria of any sort. But this implies the abandonment of any attempt to evaluate beliefs. Instrumentalism, in a word, implies the nihilistic conclusion that the elaborate arguments by which human beings sometimes defend their beliefs mask the real reasons—or more accurately the social, psychological, and glandular influences that determine belief.

Even in a thoroughly naturalized epistemology, doubts will arise and be resolved. But inquiry in this sense will be understood as the adjustment of an organism to its environment through the discarding, addition, and reinforcement of beliefs. But the change or retention of a belief as a result of inquiry will be nothing more than a subtle manifestation of the adjustment of an organism to its environment.

There is something in all of these notions. Human beings do not wait upon philosophical criticism to form and express beliefs, nor is it reasonable to dismiss as unjustified all the beliefs for which no satisfactory philosophical account has been provided. But it is one thing to acknowledge that belief and even inquiry precede formulation and application of criteria, and another to reject all standards of belief.

Another version of instrumentalism continues to employ the same criteria that are customarily employed at the experiential level but invokes instrumentalism to "justify" the adoption of these criteria. We believe that nature is regular because that belief helps us cope, but once we accept this and other criterial beliefs, we argue like everyone else. The multitude of human ends makes this possibility relativistic: those whose principal purpose is power over their natural and social environment will invoke different criteria and therefore reach different results from those who aim at contemplation of nature and community with their fellow human beings. And the fact that beliefs can be valued for their own sake means that the instrumentalistic character of this version of pragmatism will not make much difference; if it is possible to value one's identity as a Christian or a Marxist, then the distinction between instrumentalist and noninstrumentalist relativism will not be very large. And the remarks made previously about the nihilistic implications of a thoroughly naturalized epistemology will continue to hold true.

SECOND INTERPRETATION: MIGHT AS RIGHT

The central problem for pragmatism as so far expounded is that of multiple ends. Some people prefer excitement to security; others prefer security to excitement. Others defy the pragmatist ban and seek Truth for its own sake. And once this end is admitted as a possible one, the pragmatist position collapses. For those who seek Truth can condemn the pragmatist as in error, whereas the pragmatist can only regard Truth seekers as different from himself. (Though he might still use rhetoric to destroy the credibility of the seeker after Truth.)

One way out of this impasse is to point out that any investigator, in order to pursue his inquiries, must survive—and enjoy the leisure, resources, and opportunities for discussion necessary for inquiry. Hence ideas inconsistent with physical survival or continued membership in the community of scholars can be rejected on pragmatic grounds. And those who control the levers of power within the larger society, or within the academic world, have the ability to establish what have been called "conversational constraints." Breach of these constraints will lead to one's exclusion, physical or moral, from those situations in which inquiry is alone possible.

We have thus reached the pragmatism of Callicles, as developed in the *Gorgias*: might makes right, and those who assert standards of Truth not supported by power are idle dreamers whose fantasies can be dispelled by appropriate use of the instruments of coercion. To "speak power to truth," as a political scientist friend of mine once put it, is the most (and in the end the only) effective way of settling disputes.

It is important not to view this position too crudely. Shooting dissident intellectuals or dismissing them from academic positions is only the simplest way of bringing power to bear upon the life of the mind. There are many other methods of making a position seem unthinkable by social pressure and psychological manipulation, with direct physical or economic coercion only as a last resort.[7]

I am not arguing here for a conspiracy theory. The ways in which the world makes some conclusions seem plausible and others incredible are often enough manipulated by this or that group promoting this or that end. But they normally work in a decentralized, half-conscious manner, and their effect is importantly felt within the would-be rebel himself.

Nor am I arguing that pragmatists have sinister purposes. I have every reason to believe their goals are such as I would approve: the preservation and extension of the central goods of Western civilization. But even the most well-meaning program can develop a sinister dimension, and the pragmatic tradition is singularly ill-prepared to guard itself against degeneration into something very much like totalitarianism.

"Might is right" should not be understood as a criterion directly employed in deciding what to believe, or even as a second-order criterion supporting a decision to use a particular set of criteria. It rather endorses the (often half-conscious) processes by which individuals adapt themselves to the demands of those who control the conditions of their existence, and by which rare individuals seize opportunities for power outside traditional channels. This reading circumvents some of the awkward questions pressed against such positions by Plato, such as who actually is powerful and how he knows what is in his interest. But it also represents a return, by another route, to the thoroughly naturalized epistemology just discussed.

But the question, Who has power? is not merely theoretical; it arises quite quickly in practical contexts. Socrates was killed by the people of Athens, but he deeply shaped the intellectual and cultural life of subsequent generations. Lenin's revolution triumphed, but—or so many historians believe—he would have been horrified by its outcome. Hitler ruled murderously for a while, but his rule was in the end destroyed, and there is reason to suppose that it was inherently self-destructive. Louis XV enjoyed power, wealth, and glory and was content to leave to his successor the consequences of his rule. Which if any of these men enjoyed power in the fullest sense is an inevitable question. We must also ask about the subtler forms of power enjoyed by those, frequently lowly, persons who are charged with the care of small children: since their influence on the next generation can be immense, some way has to be found of comparing their power with the more conventional forms wielded by politicians. And the attempt to answer these questions poses the further question, Which of the ends human beings set for themselves is the most worthy of pursuit?

Hence "might makes right" cannot long remain a mere unconscious adaptation to the realities of power. It requires reflection on the nature of power and on that of the good life for human beings.

Moreover, "might makes right" normally, though by no means invariably, leads to conventionalism: to the acceptance of the standards supported by the forces dominant within one's society. But "might makes right" is offensive to conventional opinion, which requires more support for its principles than the shifting history of power relations provides. (That is why Hobbes came to be known as the Monster of Malmesbury.)

Nor is the situation altered when the slogan is invoked by a revolutionary movement sure of its coming triumph, as Mao proclaimed that political power comes from a barrel of a gun. For some of the supporters of the movement will die before it triumphs, and some will be asked to die in its behalf. For either of these the power of the movement will not provide sufficient support for its norms. And in fact no movement or institution is able to distribute rewards and penalties efficiently enough to be able to rely on them alone to sustain itself.

The same is true for matters thought of as more intellectual than political. The scientific community rewards creative work and penalizes fraud. But it cannot guarantee that even the most diligent labor will produce creative work or that the best creative work will receive recognition. Nor can it guarantee that fraud will always be detected. The investigator's devotion to scientific truth will therefore remain an essential element in the scientific enterprise.

There remains the question whether human beings are capable of pursuing Truth independently of other interests. In part, this issue is resolved by the example of those men and women who have sacrificed their lives and other interests for the sake of Truth as they understood it. But it also helps if one thinks of Truth, not as a value-free "objective" reality of the positivist sort, but as in some respects like a person with whom one can enter into a relationship of friendship. Or rather, even the harsh side of Truth seeking, that summed up in phrases like "facing reality," must be understood in personal terms, as the justice or severe mercy of a transcendent Judge.

THIRD INTERPRETATION: THE SOVEREIGNTY OF THE GOOD

Another interpretation of pragmatism allows a breach in the pragmatist unwillingness to attribute objective value or Truth to anything; even the pragmatist rejection of absolutes turns out, on this interpretation, not to be an absolute. One state of affairs—call it the Good—is allowed to be treated as valuable regardless of human purposes and conventions. And other states of affairs, including those in which human beings assert propositions, are evaluated according to their contribution to it. Although any state of affairs whatever could play this role, the candidate for the Good that least violates the spirit of pragmatism is the ongoing conversation among human beings that goes by the name of "civilization."

In order to avoid an infinite regress, some states of affairs must be valued, not as means to civilization, but as components of it. The judgment that asserting a proposition contributes to the advance of civilization and is for that reason correct must sometimes rest on a judgment that the assertion of that proposition of itself participates in the Good and that for that reason the proposition is True.

Sometimes P must be recognized, without the bringing to bear of any further criterion, as contributing, that is, participating in, the Good. Otherwise the proposition that "P contributes to the Good" must be read as "'P contributes to the Good' contributes to the Good," and so on indefinitely.

I have so far accepted the premise that the Good may be identified with the continued conversation that constitutes our civilization. But sometimes that civilization has been advanced by acts of grave injustice—or so it appears. Hence we must accept one of two propositions: (1) the pursuit of justice is itself a constituent part of the conversation that forms our civilization, so that injustice of itself constitutes a lapse from the Good; or (2) the furtherance of civilization is only one good among others, not, as the present interpretation supposes, *the* Good. In either case, pragmatism will have passed over into its Platonist opponent.

One way of representing the Good that is the standard of Truth is as that which is in accord with the judgments of a perfect Judge. But, in representing our conclusion in this way, we seem to have reached the limits of philosophy. For philosophy is the attempt to say clearly whatever can be said clearly, and the perfect Judge is an object of imaginative representation: whether one of the private representations that constitute poetry or one of the public representations that form the stuff of religion. The final step in my argument is therefore to explain the nature of religious representations and what it means for such a representation to manifest Truth. But before reaching this stage of the argument, it is necessary to explore further the relativistic and nihilistic possibilities that the arguments of this chapter have raised.

4

RELATIVISM

THE NEXT RIVAL TO A Platonic conception of Truth that must be considered is relativism, according to which there is no Truth, but rather a multitude of truths, corresponding to the multitude of frameworks within which human beings attempt to conduct their lives.

THE CONCEPT OF A FRAMEWORK

I take the essence of relativism to be that reasoning is possible only when assumptions are shared and that there is a plurality of possible sets of assumptions among whose adherents no argument is possible. Crucial to relativism, thus conceived, is the existence of basic standards that underlie the assertions human beings make. Philosophers who have taken relativism seriously—or whose work raises relativistic possibilities—have given the sources of such standards various names.[1] I here settle on the word *frameworks*.

Frameworks have the following five features:

1. They are not assertions or sets of assertions; otherwise they would be subject to criteria of assessment.
2. They are central to the ways human beings act: how human beings of all sorts conduct their daily lives and how scientists conduct observations and experiments.

3. They are often tacit and, in any case, not wholly and adequately expressible in ordinary prose.
4. They are embedded in groups, which teach and uphold them by nonrational means, including exercise of parental authority and boycott campaigns directed at intellectual deviants.
5. Frameworks transcend the fact/value distinction; for they determine what is to count as a fact, partly in terms of the interests or ideals that prompt the discourse in question, and shape the methods of investigation used by their adherents.

Thus a framework can be defined as a collection of methods and habits of thought and action that determines what those who adhere to it regard as good and true.

The relationship between a framework and a statement supported by it can be compared to the relationship between a legal system and a statement of law. The analogy with law focuses attention on one important aspect of the concept of a framework: frameworks are not merely abstract sets of norms but have a history of development and decay. But the relativist will stress two aspects of legal systems above others: that their validity is limited to a particular territory or system of courts and that it is possible that an agent will be subject to two different legal systems, which impose incompatible requirements upon him.

The analogy also helps explain how, even if relativism is true, no attempt at a framework one might try to formulate is tenable. A framework is not the mere creation of an individual consciousness but exists only because the standards it proposes are or can be upheld by some group. This *because* is at once logical and causal. It is logical, inasmuch as a set of ideas counts as a framework only if it provides standards that transcend the impressions of a particular person at a particular time. But it is also causal, since the conceptual features of "framework" arise from a need to describe phenomena observed among human beings, and these include transmission mechanisms within the purview of social psychology.

But the social dimension of the concept of a framework has to be qualified in two ways. First, relativism is not individualistic subjectivism, for which anything goes intellectually; nor is it collective subjectivism, which would settle intellectual questions by voting. The analogy with law makes this point clear: although law exists in relation to a particular society, law and public opinion are not the same. At least in the view of most legal scholars, "anything goes" does not apply to legal argument: the precedents and statutes have to be taken into account. But one can say, so long as one does not do so too often, that the decisions of the courts, even those of the last resort, are legally and not just morally and politically wrong. Likewise a moral relativist who finds his basic standards in the ethos of a given society can disagree with the majority of that society (though perhaps not with an overwhelming majority) on some moral issue, so long as he is prepared to defend his disagreement on grounds the majority is prepared to accept. In brief, although the standards we employ are (according to the relativist) grounded in their acceptance by a group to which we belong, the application of these standards is objective and not a matter of what people think.

Second, although an ordinary person must choose (if that is the word) among the frameworks he encounters in his social environment, an extraordinary individual will be able to create a new framework and induce others to adhere to his standards. But any framework must at least be capable of being taught to others, as well as applied in a consistent fashion by those who adhere to it.

The analogy with law is also helpful in understanding the problems involved in applying frameworks other than one's own. The testimony of the law is somewhat divided on this point. Federal courts exercising diversity jurisdiction (though here the judge himself may be subject to the system of law he is applying), courts applying foreign law in conflicts-of-law cases, and colonial courts applying native customary law all do something very much like interpreting an alien framework. On the other hand, it is a central principle of the American law of religion that courts will not, in settling property disputes arising from ecclesiastical schism, attempt to adjudicate the theological issues.[2]

Another set of problems may be compared with the problems posed by rebellion, civil war, revolution, coup d'état, foreign invasion, and formation of governments in exile.[3] To these may be added the schisms that are a frequent affliction of churches and voluntary political associations. The point of the analogy between the clash of frameworks and institutional schisms is not that the rival groups necessarily employ different frameworks, but that when such a schism takes place there now are two or more sets of criteria of legitimacy where there once was one. What the relativist is concerned with are situations in which there appears to be, as a result of the existence of a plurality of frameworks, a plurality of incompatible truths about the same subject matter. And this interest includes cases in which what started as a divergence of application of the same standards has turned into a divergence in the standards applied, what may be called a "conceptual schism."[4]

The analogy between a framework and a legal system also puts in question the association frequently made between relativism and tolerance. There is no reason to suppose that those administering a legal system will tolerate a rival legal system established within their jurisdiction. Likewise relativists need be no more tolerant than others and have special reasons for being intolerant; if argument is impossible, coercion is specially attractive.

But decentralized systems of common law, or the unspoken conventions of which the members of a society are not aware until they are violated, are a better analogy to frameworks than a developed legal system. Frameworks are usually not deliberately adopted, modified, or abandoned, nor is there usually an authority charged with making final determinations about their application to difficult cases. Explicit teaching, or formal repudiation of deviant modes of thought and practice, is a sign that a framework is already under stress. The teaching of a framework takes place more by example than by precept, and nonvoluntary acquisition rather than deliberate choice. When a choice takes place, as in cases of religious conversion, it is more a matter of a person's assent to what has happened to him without his will than it is his decision to replace one stock of ideas with another.

FURTHER PRELIMINARIES

One objection to relativism is that it immediately proves incoherent, since the relativist cannot, in his own terms, assert its truth. The argument goes as follows:

1. The relativist is committed to treating all statements as elliptical, that is, as containing a suppressed reference to the standards of some group.
2. And that commitment extends to statements about frameworks and the relationship between a framework and statements made within it.

So:

3. The relativist's attempt to make statements of any sort will lead to an infinite regress, much as if he always read "p" as "I believe that p."

And

4. In particular he will not be able to assert his own relativism.

But the relativist can deny (1). Relativism as here presented does not assert that all statements are to be expanded to read, "According to framework F, p." On the contrary, the relativist asserts that all statements must be made *within* a framework, which need not be treated as part of the statement itself. All statements must be made in a language, but that does not mean that all statements must be prefaced with "in language L."

Some critics of relativism have argued that a relativist cannot maintain the usual sense of "true," or the prescriptive force of moral judgments, while admitting that positions other than his own are, from an equally valid point of view, true or well grounded.[5] But the relativist need not concede any such status to statements made in frameworks other than his own: as he uses words, *true* or *well grounded* engages criteria characteristic of his framework. He will also maintain, however, that other frameworks are possible, that generate senses of "true" or "well grounded" analogous to his (he may himself use the word *orthodoxy* to describe them; compare the section Terminological Issues in chapter 1); and that no rational argument is available to show that his own (or his opponent's) position is true or preferable. He may attempt to persuade his opponents to accept his framework and govern their lives accordingly. But he will not use rational persuasion in this attempt: he will not argue with unbelief but only preach to it.[6]

A final preliminary issue is the status of the articulate presentations of frameworks whose construction is one of the traditional tasks of philosophy. Since frameworks are not assertions or systems of assertions, such theories do not themselves assert frameworks (they at most display them). Rather they are at one remove from the framework itself. Accordingly, they can be true or false, even if the relativist is right. But, if he is right, they can only represent or fail to represent the framework that inspires them. Such articulations are important when it is proposed to subject a framework to critical scrutiny, and for that reason traditionalists sometimes resist the attempt to formulate their frameworks, though at the cost of making their commitments vulnerable to silent rejection.

THE RELATIVIST ARGUMENT

The core of the relativist's contention can be summed up in the following five theses:

1. Whenever someone makes an assertion, he presupposes some standard, according to which his assertion is to be judged true or false, and on which its intelligibility depends.
2. People have employed incompatible standards in making assertions about the same subject matter.
3. Sometimes these differences of standard are ultimate. That is to say, there is sometimes no further standard to which appeal can be made in order to determine which of the rival standards is correct.
4. Where the condition described in (3) obtains, it is nonsense to speak of one set of standards as correct. Such fundamental standards can only be described.

Hence:

5. A decision to accept or reject some fundamental standard, to the extent that it lies within our power, must of necessity be arbitrary.

The frameworks just discussed are the sources of fundamental standards, in the sense of thesis (3).

It seems to me that theses (1) and (2) are true, and that theses (4) and (5) follow from (1) through (3). The truth or falsity of relativism thus depends on that of (3). I postpone discussion of thesis (3) and concentrate, in the present section, on that of the other four theses.

Thesis (1)

Thesis (1) asserts that the first question to be asked of an utterance is by what criteria it invites judgment. If there are no criteria for an utterance's truth, it is not a statement but an emotional outpouring, an aesthetic performance, a vocal exercise, or some other kind of nonassertive speech act. If the criteria for the truth of an utterance, except for background criteria such as competence in the language used, are the same as those for its sincerity, then it is a report of the utterer's subjective state. Only if a standard can be judged true or false by another person, employing criteria other than the subject's sincerity, do we have a statement capable of truly describing the public world.[7] (In practice, this distinction is not sharp. For if an avowal of pain is widely discordant with the observed facts, we will be led to question the speaker's sincerity.)

One persistent problem for relativism is to prevent collapse into subjectivism.[8] Since for the relativist a criterion rests on a collective or individual decision, or an unwilled inability to think otherwise, it might seem that such criteria can be abandoned or modified at any time. If so, they will fail to function as criteria and our intellectual life will turn out to have no rules. In fact the relativist's criteria will exhibit no more, but also no less, resistance to change than any well-entrenched feature of our individual or collective lives. Merely describing a practice may not provide a very satisfying answer to philosophical questions, but if the practice is *our* practice this response will have to suffice in the absence of some showing that another answer is available. Nor does talk of intuition change the situation, since an intuition is nothing but a clear and lively propensity to believe, whose claim to disclose a universally accessible reality at least requires defense against the relativist's argument.

In applying thesis (1), it is necessary to distinguish between strict and weak (or presumptive) criteria. Strict criteria are necessary and sufficient conditions of those statements of which they are criteria; weak or presumptive criteria only provide reasons for making the statements in question, in the absence of evidence to the contrary. Weak or presumptive criteria satisfy thesis (1), so long as they are determinate enough to meet the needs of actual use.

One might attempt to evade thesis (1) in two ways: by doing without criteria altogether or by shifting the locus of epistemological interest from justification to criticism. The abandonment of criteria means subjectivism, whether overt or concealed. Overt subjectivism is no problem for the epistemologist: if someone prefers not to engage in disciplined intellectual activity, it is not the task of the philosopher to force him to do so, only to point out that the cost of abandoning criteria is abandoning the concept of truth. Covert subjectivism needs only to be exposed as such. A shift from justification to criticism does nothing to eliminate the need for criteria, though the criteria required are negative rather than positive, determining when a claim has been refuted rather than when it has been confirmed.

Thesis (2)

I therefore shall take thesis (1) as established. It is important to see that thesis (2) asserts something more than a diversity of customary moralities, or ways of judging. What it says is not merely that individuals and groups have held incompatible convictions, but that the standards individuals and groups apply in making their incompatible assessments are themselves incompatible.

De facto ethical relativity has a special importance for relativism generally, since we at least appear to have for ethics, as opposed to science or theology, a palpable criterion of disagreement independent of the rival positions. If two people find themselves on opposite sides of an election, or of a barricade, it is hard for them to pretend that the difference between them is not real. Even here, however, we may have Hobbesian conflict, in which two people attempt to frustrate and even kill one another, without claiming to be in the right by any standard the other might accept or even understand.

It is unnecessary to have recourse to primitive societies or alien cultures in order to discover controversial standards of morally acceptable conduct or acceptable belief. There are many conflicts in Western culture that seem irresolvable. And in disciplines such as physics and history, inquirers work with norms of rational belief that dictate what weight, if any, is to be given items of supposed evidence. And communities of inquirers adopt common norms and regard those who stray from them as "cranks," to be excluded from participation in the life of the community (compare the section An Example:

Psychical Research in chapter 1). The core relativist doctrine is that, in such cases, the notion of truth, about physics as much as about ethics, is relative to the intellectual and social framework and that alternative frameworks are not wrong but different.

Theses (4) and (5)

I now take theses (1) and (2) as established and argue that, if thesis (3) is also true, theses (4) and (5) follow. Imagine frameworks F and F^*, of which it is the case that there is no standard by which appeal can be made to determine which is adequate to reality or more nearly so.

It follows immediately that one cannot assert that F (or F^*) provides the proper standard. By thesis (1), such an indication of preference would not be an assertion. It also follows that there is no other way in which F can be judged superior to F^*. Even "reasons of the heart" do not provide a way out of the impasse, since, given (1) through (3), no grounds can be found for choice between a consoling framework and one that gives a sense of facing unpleasant realities without flinching (see further the section First Interpretation: A Relativism of Multiple Ends in chapter 3). In other words, given (1) through (3), (4) and (5) follow.

RELATIVISM ASSESSED

It is now time to confront the central issue between the relativist and his opponent, that of the truth or falsity of thesis (3). We must ask whether it is in fact the case that some or all differences of standard preclude settlement of differences of opinion by rational means; whether the no-argument points we appear to reach in talking to one another are in fact ultimate. I begin with a discussion of some inadequate arguments against thesis (3) and then argue that neither thesis (3) nor its negation can be established directly by philosophical argument.[9]

The first inadequate argument may be called the *leaky boat argument*.[10] It supposes that, insofar as the conditions pointed to by thesis (2) obtain, these conflicts can be regarded as the result of bias on one or both sides of the dispute. And it maintains, for some dimensions of our intellectual life at least, that this bias can be reduced to negligible proportions. All boats leak, but some boats leak more than others. And not all boats sink.

But the leaky boat argument confuses relativism and subjectivism. The point of the relativist argument is not that cognition expresses personal or collective bias, rather that the procedures that historians or scientists employ to eliminate such biases reflect an understanding of the world and the inquirer's place in it and that such an understanding is beyond the reach of rational argument (see An Example: Psychical Research, chapter 1).

Another argument against thesis (3) may be called the *common world argument*. One form of this argument—attributable to the philosopher G. E. Moore—points out simple facts about our shared environment to which we will all agree. And the common world argument is available in ethics as well: as all of us will agree, death, maiming, and pain are evils, whose infliction requires some sort of justification.

But the common world argument is not persuasive. Simple beliefs about the common world do not in fact receive universal assent, though denying some of them might risk confinement in an asylum. Moreover, one can maintain that truth is framework-relative, while conceding that for a range of propositions nearly all frameworks coincide. Disputes about the assassination of John Kennedy engage deep assumptions about, for example, the role of conspiracy in history, but no one thinks he escaped death and is now living in Argentina.

A more challenging version of the common world argument holds that, even in order to recognize disagreement, we must work from a body of agreement.[11] In order to understand what someone is saying, we have to translate what he says into our own language in such a way that, for the vast bulk of cases, we assign to the sentences of a speaker conditions of truth that (in our view) actually obtain. When we do ascribe a false belief to a speaker, we do so in the light of considerations of simplicity, hunches about the effects of social conditioning, and knowledge of explainable error, as acquired from our own cases as well as that of others.

Let it be granted that we would be unable to translate a language whose users' judgments did not in some respects agree with our own. We still have to ask whether we can recognize that a group is speaking a language when we are unable to translate statements of that language into our own.

Suppose a group of technologically superior aliens were to invade the Earth. As is customary in such situations, they employ their technology to destroy our way of life and subject us to their will. We observe these creatures' uttering noises in one another's direction, handing one another pieces of paper with marks on them, and so forth. But, try as we may, we are never able to correlate these sounds and markings with the actions of the aliens and objects in our common world in such a way that an alien-English dictionary could be compiled.

One might ask how we know that the alien "language" is used to make assertions or that the aliens have a concept of truth and falsity. Our evidence on this point is indirect: since their language seems to function satisfactorily for them, we assume that it must be at least as rich as our own in forms of expression. But it seems a fair conclusion that if the aliens do have a concept of truth and falsity, it bears only a remote analogy to ours. For the categories and criteria in terms of which they apply their notion of truth will bear only a distant relationship to ours. In other words, their statements depend for their intelligibility on a radically different background than do ours.

Yet the aliens' language could be translatable in principle. To prove that it is not would involve establishing a negative of a sort that cannot be established. Still, without being untranslatable in principle, a language might be untranslatable within the life expectancy of the human species.

Furthermore, the aliens' language might be only partially translatable. We might be able to understand a few alien sentences, without being ever able to understand the vast bulk of their speech. And it often seems that we human beings can understand one another and then reach a blank wall, a point of no argument and no understanding. The possibility of partial intertranslatability also explains how people employing different frameworks can understand one another well enough to establish the fact of conflict, in other words, how conflicting standards can deal with the same subject matter.

Many aspects of our life together are characterized by the coexistence, peaceful or otherwise, of heterogeneous principles. Such principles can be ranked or weighted in more than one way, and it may be that between rankings and weightings no impartial judgment is possible. If so, adherents of rival rankings and weightings, and of frameworks based on such weightings and rankings, and of frameworks built upon such weightings and rankings, will be able to argue with one another about the application of shared principles. But there will come a point at which argument and mutual understanding reach a blank wall. In such contexts the claims of relativism will be very persuasive, especially if the relativist concedes that conflicting frameworks may overlap somewhat.

A third group of arguments against thesis (3) attempts to find some point outside all frameworks, or necessarily common to them all, that provides a basis for their acceptance or rejection. What we are looking for here is norms binding upon all rational beings, which will determine or place limits on the frameworks they can accept. But either the proposed norm will be a hypothetical imperative, so that one can evade its force by indifference to the end proposed, or it will be a categorical imperative and rejected by some people.

The most plausible hypothetical imperatives of the understanding are those that tell us how to secure our own survival and that of the groups with which we identify. Thus, it may be argued, the acceptance or retention of a framework is rational just in case it contributes to the survival of the individual or group that proposes to employ the framework in question. But survival is not the only end individuals and groups have, and both individuals and groups sometimes prefer extinction to the sacrifice of some treasured belief or practice. Hence instrumentalism is a relativistic doctrine, since it makes rationality and truth depend on the ends set for themselves by the individuals and groups making the inquiry (see First Interpretation: A Relativism of Multiple Ends, chapter 3).

A plausible categorical imperative of the understanding is the principle of (non)contradiction. But just as some moralists hold that moral rationality consists in knowing when to violate even the most basic moral rules, so some thinkers hold that rationality includes selective self-contradiction. Thus some theologians, to the great scandal of professors of philosophy, have claimed the privilege of holding and teaching self-contradictory doctrines.

The principle of self-contradiction is best read as a hypothetical imperative: if one wishes to make assertions, these assertions must exclude other assertions (their negations). One can evade the principle of contradiction only by ceasing to make statements: the same may be said of the requirement that all assertions involve the application of some standard or criterion. And a charitable interpretation of the theologians just referred to is that they hold that mysteries such as the Trinity and the Incarnation cannot be expressed in assertions, but only through self-contradictory formulae that supply the conditions of acceptable Christian discourse (see Religion Defined, chapter 7). But the employment of the principle of contradiction depends on assumptions about the meaning of words and sentences that are not compelled by a commitment to making assertions. Otherwise one could always extricate oneself from a supposed contradiction by making a meaningless distinction. If, as is plausible, the distinction between sense and nonsense is framework-dependent, so, in its application, will be the principle of self-contradiction.

Some philosophers have supposed that we have a mode of contact with the world independent of any cognitive system and that this contact provides a criterion that can be brought to bear on any belief, regardless of framework. The concept of "non-epistemic seeing" provides an example of such supposed contact.[12] If by non-epistemic seeing is meant the capacity shared by human beings and, say, chickens, it provides no escape from the problem of relativism. It is easy to imagine rational beings whose physical structure, and thus whose perception of their environment, is very different from our own, who would consequently employ very different standards in making judgments about that environment. If, on the other hand, nonepistemic seeing is defined as a kind of seeing that lacks epistemic implications, then it follows immediately that such seeing has no epistemological importance.

A final attempt to refute thesis (3) is the *critical argument* advanced by Sir Karl Popper and his disciples, which attempts to define a standpoint that can be used to judge all frameworks because it is not committed to any particular belief. Instead, adherents of the critical approach resolve to subject all their beliefs and attitudes to critical scrutiny. And they claim that they can subject the critical argument itself, and their own critical practice, to critical scrutiny as well.

But since adherents of the critical argument have intellectual argument in mind (and not such activities as experimentation with drugs that, their adherents claim, free the mind from the repressive categories of Western civilization),[13] it seems that they are at least committed to the laws of logic. A proposal to reject logic would have to employ logic, and the complex argument such a proposal would require could always be handled by the contention that there was something wrong with one's logical apparatus, but not with logic as such. That is how problems such as Russell's paradox are, in fact, handled.

All attempts to refute thesis (3) have failed, but thesis (3) has not thereby been established. I now argue that there is no way of establishing thesis (3); in other words, that it is possible that all frameworks but one can be eliminated. Criteria for the acceptability of frameworks can be drawn from the concept of a framework itself, a concept the relativist cannot reject, since the argument for relativism (and indeed the very articulation of the relativist's position) requires him to use it. It is of the essence of a framework that it is a source of standards of truth, usable by more than one person and by the same person on more than one occasion. And some frameworks break down, because they cannot function in the way the relativist requires them to function.

In discussing the breakdown of frameworks, it is useful to distinguish between frameworks that have received philosophical articulation and those that exist only as modes of practice. In the former case, one can apply the framework to itself; in the latter, one has to rely on less rigorous modes of argument, placing the framework in historical context and explaining how unexpected events might subject it to an intolerable strain. For example, a framework may remain tenable only because its adherents are prevented from acting on it, as is the case with a political perspective that survives only because those who employ it are kept out of power.

In any event, frameworks can break down in a number of ways. They can counsel or imply their own rejection. They can be inapplicable to problems that their adherents cannot, in their own terms, evade or dismiss. They contain principles that pull in such different directions that they can be applied only if favorable circumstances protect the adherents of the framework from the tensions within their ideas. Such favorable circumstances may be vulnerable to forces released by the adherents of the framework as they act in accordance with it. A framework can be preserved from breakdown only because the evaluations it embodies are not generally enacted within its adherent's society. The mere preponderance of evidence cannot lead us to abandon one framework for another, since what is accepted as evidence depends on one's framework. But one way a framework can break down is by being incapable of accounting for what it requires its adherents to accept as evidence.

Not all frameworks, therefore, are acceptable. But to establish that there is only one acceptable framework, one would have to establish (*a*) that there is at least one such framework, and that not all frameworks refute themselves; and (*b*) that there is at most one such framework, and that all frameworks but (at most) one refute themselves. It should be clear that neither (*a*) nor (*b*) can be established.

What (*a*) asks is that a framework should guarantee its own consistency. One reason for thinking that this requirement cannot be met may be found in the mathematician Kurt Gödel's celebrated proof that the consistency of arithmetic cannot be established without recourse to methods of argument whose consistency is at least as open to doubt as that of arithmetic itself. And, Gödel apart, what (*a*) requires is that we anticipate circumstances and predict that none of them will subject our framework to intolerable strain. It should be clear that this is not possible.

The only way of showing that (*b*) is the case starts with some framework we deem most basic, show that it is self-destructive and thus work our way through various possible frameworks one by one. And what this (broadly Hegelian) strategy requires is, first, that some framework be identified as the most basic and, second, that when a framework breaks down, there be one and only one successor framework, to which we then give our attention. Without some sequence of this sort, it is hard to see how one could ever claim to have exhausted all the possible frameworks. But, even if the first requirement is meant, the second cannot be, whether frameworks are considered primarily as sets of propositions or primarily as modes of practice.

If a set of internally consistent propositions $P_1, P_2, P_3, \ldots P_n$ is inconsistent, there will be not one but up to n ways of restoring it to consistency. Children who find their parents' way of life insupportable react to it in not one but many ways, up to as many different ways as there are children. And when a given form of society breaks down, it can do so in not one but many ways.

In addition, since the interpretation of a framework must in the last resort lie with those who adhere to it, one cannot conclude too quickly that a given framework has been refuted.

One should not underestimate the ingenuity of human beings in repairing their frameworks in the face of seemingly devastating criticism. Major traditions such as Christianity and Marxism are best thought of as consisting not of one, but of a family of frameworks, not refuted until every member of the family has fallen. And it seems plausible, as a historical matter, that no such family of frameworks has been refuted, although some of them have lost their vitality for reasons external to rational argument. On the other hand, people have continued to adhere to frameworks that are no longer rationally defensible, for example, because their social situation does not permit them to accept the consequences of the rejection of such frameworks.

I have appealed to the notion of internal criticism in order to establish that at least some frameworks can rationally be rejected. But it might be argued, in the light of the remarks just made, that the very notion of internal criticism is unacceptable. For it supposes that there are standards for the interpretation and application of frameworks, independent of their actual employment by their adherents.[14] So long as the adherents of a framework continue to employ it, that outsiders find it incoherent indicates only that they are outsiders.

But any framework must make possible the notion of the misapplication of a norm, and with it of the carelessness or inattention that may cause such a misapplication. The mere continued application of the norms generated by a framework does not establish more than a presumption against the view that the framework continues in operation only because its adherents misapply its standards and the correct application of a framework is to reject it.

Some might argue that, even if we cannot show that all frameworks but one break down, the possibility that a framework may break down contains all that is required to refute thesis (3). For thesis (3) asserts that there is sometimes *no* further standard to which appeal can be made to settle disputes, and the possibility of breakdown provides such a standard even if it cannot be applied to resolve all cases. This argument raises the issue of how effective a criterion must be to function as such for the purposes of thesis (1). Though necessary and sufficient conditions are not required, some degree of practical usefulness is still necessary. And, for all that the preceding arguments indicate, there may be a wide variety of frameworks, none of which will ever break down. Hence it seems insufficient to rely on the bare possibility of breakdown to refute relativism.

We must proceed in many practical contexts as if relativism were true. For (whatever may be the case ultimately) our intellectual world comprises a multitude of warring factions, each of which has had the opportunity to hear all the arguments the others present. And there are no particular reasons to suppose that further discussion will, in fact, lead to a greater degree of agreement on contested issues. On the contrary, such discussions tend to produce further divisions, as interaction with group A splits group B into two further factions, groups B_1 and B_2, according to their divergent responses to such interaction. (Consider, for example, the divisive impact of feminism on the Christian churches.)

On the other hand, it is impossible to prove that these divisions would not yield to further experience and rational argument, if the adherents of the rival frameworks were only to think things through calmly. And failure to convince may arise not from irrationality on either side but simply from lack of imagination in seeking out arguments. In such a context, the idea of Truth can function as a regulative ideal, moving us to restrain impulses toward relativistic intolerance and to look for new arguments when old ones have proved unsuccessful. As such an ideal, the notion of Truth belongs to the same family of ideas as the concept of God, which also functions in this manner in the philosophy of Kant. And this is how it should be, since one way of specifying the notion of Truth is as the way God sees the world.

Moreover, the relativist can hardly dismiss this notion of Truth as a pretty fiction. For, according to his arguments, believers in Truth cannot be in error (at most they are different from himself). Believers in Truth, on the other hand, can, consistently with their position, regard relativists as in error. But before exploring this argument further, it is necessary to consider a thoroughgoing nihilism, which denies even the degree of order relativists find in our intellectual lives.

5

NIHILISM

NIHILISM—AND IN PARTICULAR the nihilism said to be characteristic of the present age—is much talked about, especially by philosophers of a Continental persuasion. But even the most careful discussions tend to be unclear on the issue of what nihilism exactly is.[1] And until we grasp the question of what nihilism exactly is, we are in no position to decide whether it is a peculiarly modern problem or a perpetual human one. Nor can we effectively evaluate various strategies—individual and collective—for attempting to escape it, if indeed escape is possible or desirable.

VARIETIES OF NIHILISM

A first approximation to a definition of nihilism is that the nihilist believes that nothing matters. If this sort of nihilist is right, I have no reason to prefer pleasure to pain, life to death, knowledge to ignorance, virtue to vice, or beauty to ugliness. Nor do I have any reason to reverse conventional evaluations and prefer, say, pain to pleasure.

Let us try to spell the issue out. I do not only experience certain desires, enjoyments, and retrospective feelings of satisfaction and regret: I also employ principles of evaluation in order to resolve contradictions among my desires. The nihilist cannot extinguish my desires or aversions: what he can perhaps do is abolish my principles of evaluation and leave me to my feelings.

Two sorts of cases are to be distinguished. Jane masturbates and feels guilty afterward. She might persuade herself that masturbation is bad and give up the habit or persuade herself that it is good and stop feeling guilty. Nihilism deprives her of both options, insofar as they involve judgments of value, and leaves her to both her habit and her guilt. T. E. Lawrence does not like the fact that he likes killing. Nihilism forbids him either to renounce his taste for blood as morally bad or to conclude that there is nothing wrong with it.

But here we encounter a logical problem that will plague all our attempts to formulate nihilism clearly. If Jane decides to solve her problem, one way or another, the nihilist is in no position to complain. Certainly it does not follow from nihilist premises that she is under any obligation, intellectual or moral, to leave her problem unresolved.

Human beings have various ways of dealing with conflicts within and among themselves. A selection of such methods includes the confessional, drunkenness, elections, litigation, and reasoned argument. A nihilist neither should nor coherently can deny the richness and complexity of these practices. What he wants to do is to take a standpoint external to all of them and to pronounce on all of them the following judgments: first, that although they may *end* conflicts, in the sense that killing all the parties will end a conflict, none of them can in any proper sense *settle* them; and, second, that none of these methods, especially reasoned argument, is of higher authority than the others or than some new method that might be invented tomorrow.

It is evident that any nihilist has severe problems when his doctrine is applied to itself. But before exploring this issue, I should like to distinguish, and set to one side, three forms of nihilism whose inconsistency is easily shown.

The first inconsistent form is *traditional* nihilism. The traditional nihilist holds that all practices and institutions should be attacked, physically or symbolically, and that those that have worth will survive.² This sort of nihilism not only supposes that some existing practices have validity and will survive the test: it also supposes, in the most traditional philosophical manner, to provide a criterion of Truth (capacity to survive the "general blowup").

Positivistic nihilism is also inconsistent. A positivistic nihilist consigns ethics, theology, religion, aesthetics, and political ideology to the flames—or, less dramatically, he regards them as cognitively meaningless. But he also believes that science, mathematics, and commonsense fact-stating discourse will survive the purging of culture that he recommends. The positivist supposes that he has a criterion of Truth independent of human purposes and conventions, that is, the canons of logic and scientific method. But the canons of conventional science are as open to nihilistic attack as those of conventional morality. And to exalt knowledge over ignorance, truth over error, and science over pseudoscience is to appeal to a hierarchy of values no less than to exalt virtue over vice.

A third inconsistent form of nihilism—what may be called *liberal* nihilism—is openly selective. Its crucial move is a distinction between the public and the private sphere. In the private sphere human beings are free to affirm, and act upon, any principles they please, even to assert the objective value of the goods they are pursuing. But they are required to respect the structures of rights defined in the public sphere, where practical reasoning is not similarly free. In the public sphere we must be neutral among the various modes of life human beings pursue. Those who assert the Truth of their private-sphere principles or demand recognition for the preferences for one sort of environment, to which their principles lead them, are rewarded with enforced silence.³

As things stand, liberal nihilism is inconsistent, for it requires that human beings act politically on no principles at all. A state that is neutral between the rest of us and someone whose self-hatred causes him to desire the destruction of the universe (or, more prosaically, the occurrence of a thermonuclear war) is paralyzed.

Liberals escape paralysis by postulating various sets of primary goods (to use the political philosopher John Rawls's expression). These goods are taken to be an exception to the general nihilism liberals espouse. But whatever the exact list of primary goods a liberal espouses, one question will always suffice to confute him. Why this set of goods and not some other; why wealth, for example, and not friendship? To answer this sort of question one must discuss what is most important in human life and why. And this is exactly the inquiry that liberalism forbids when public policy is at issue.

Furthermore, the selective nihilism involved in one sort of liberalism supposes that the public/private distinction is more absolute than it can ever be in fact. For government can never be neutral about the principles of evaluation held by those it rules: it must either accommodate or combat the religious beliefs, marriage and sexual customs, and conceptions of racial, gender, and class difference held among the population. That this is so is particularly evident in education (especially public education supported by tax money), where the government must decide to what extent to support, and to what extent to obstruct, the transmission of cultural norms from generation to generation. Those who expect our educational institutions to combat racism, but to be neutral between monogamy and promiscuity, have not learned to think consistently.

To generalize: any attempt to use nihilism to favor one mode of life, individual or collective, over another is incoherent. Nihilism regards with equal indifference martyrdom for a cause, pursuit of sensual pleasure at the risk of one's life, and the life of *l'homme moyen sensuel*. And it regards with similar indifference societies that attempt to give their members the widest possible liberty to act out their peculiar conceptions of the good life and those that attempt to protect their members from anxiety by enforcing a shared moral code. If one attempts to overcome nihilism by sheer act of will, doing the laundry is as good a remedy as cutting off one's hand.

It is now possible to confront the core problem of inconsistency inherent in the most thoroughgoing forms of nihilism.

Nihilism attempts to take a standpoint external to our practices, from which it judges them incapable of reaching Truth. But the standpoint from which such a judgment can be made and any process by which such a judgment could be reached would themselves be open to nihilistic attack. In particular the nihilist cannot claim that his nihilism expresses a superior moral or epistemic standpoint or that he knows that the pursuits of others lead only to falsehood. For his claims to Truth are as vulnerable to his skeptical strategies as are theirs.

Nietzsche makes the essential point in the following way. Under the title "The History of an Error," he traces a widening gap between appearance and Truth. He concludes: "The true world—we have abolished. What world has remained: the apparent world perhaps? But no! *With the true world we have abolished the apparent world as well.*"[4]

But the process can hardly stop here. For the distinction between things-as-they-are and things-as-they-appear is integral to things-as-they-appear. It seems to us that we are sometimes in error. And the nihilist cannot resolve this problem by denying that there is any standpoint—any "God's eye point of view," as it is sometimes called—from which human practices can be judged. For then there would be no standpoint from which he could make *this* judgment. A nihilism that hopes for coherence must adopt a less direct strategy.

The first step toward a coherent nihilism is a description of our various practices, including the ambiguities and conflicts that arise within them, and our strategies for modifying and preserving those practices in the face of challenge. The second step observes that there is not, among these practices, one that both (1) enables us to sit in judgment upon all other practices and (2) is itself free of the ambiguity and conflict that call for a higher-order practice to resolve them. The final step is a polemic, merely rhetorical in character, against any claim that one has glimpsed, even from afar, a standpoint from which one can assert transcendent Truth. Such is the practice of sophisticated nihilists in all epochs.

One way such a polemic will be carried on is through a reductive or deflationary analysis, in which the advocates of transcendent Truth are exposed as preserving and extending their own power. Nietzsche provides an example: "Supreme principle, 'God forgives those who repent,'—in plain language, those who submit to the priest."[5] (Nietzsche can hardly object to the will to power as such; his point is that the priest pretends to be doing much more than exercising power.)

DECONSTRUCTION, POLITICS, AND SEX

I now consider an important nihilist (what is usually called the *deconstructionist*) argument. This argument—possibly attributable to Wittgenstein and Derrida—rejects any attempt to place limits on the malleability of language. Any word can be used in a radically new sense; any series can be continued in a deviant way. And advocates of deconstruction go on to reject as a form of mystification the very notion of deviance (or of parasitism) in the use of language. (By *parasitism* I mean the use of language in a nonstandard way, dependent for its intelligibility upon standard use, for example sarcasm.) Neither in the world, nor in our language, nor in our other practices, nor in our individual or collective selves is there to be found a stable essence or nature capable of constraining the open texture of our concepts. Hence any language can be used to mean whatever one pleases. (The belief that such an essence or nature exists is called *essentialism*.) Hence there is no distinction between truth and error, even of the provisional sort I have called orthodoxy or correctness (Terminological Issues, chapter 1). For orthodoxy and correctness involve interpreting and applying norms accepted on authority.

More fully: any set of criteria will include two features. First it will distinguish reality from appearance, essential from accidental, and central from parasitic uses of language. Second, it will require the application of the criteria it contains in a variety of contexts, in which some persons may apply them in a way other persons regard as incorrect or deviant. But all sets of criteria will be open to multiple interpretations, first because the language in which they are expressed is open textured, and second because multiple criteria—and all conceptual schemes contain them—may sometimes conflict.

In light of these facts, the deconstructionist argues as follows. First, there is no reason to accept the judgment that minority applications of shared criteria are deviant. To draw examples from widely separated areas of life and thought, it is arbitrary to regard fictional or mythological discourse as parasitic upon fact-stating discourse or to deny the name of marriage or family to a homosexual relationship. Second, the deconstructionist questions the very distinction between the correct and the erroneous application of shared criteria, on the ground that it represents the exercise of power by some persons (the orthodox) over others (the heretics).

Defenders of conceptual orthodoxy will attempt to refute these allegations by adducing further criteria, but against all such attempts the deconstructionist can simply reiterate his fundamental strategy. The orthodox must therefore take refuge in two moves, both of which look very much like bullying. Either they will insist that it is obvious that some applications of shared criteria are erroneous or they will subject those who, in their view, misapply shared criteria to a concrete sanction, such as loss of academic employment.

One implication of the deconstructionist argument is that no distinction can be drawn between a correct and an incorrect reading of a text. Even claims to infallible authority do not escape the deconstructionist argument (if anything, they provoke it). For the pronouncements of such authority are open to endless interpretation. Still, if there is no way to limit the interpretation of a text, then the works of the deconstructionists themselves can be turned to unexpected uses, such as support for highly authoritarian solutions to our social and political problems.

A possible reading of the deconstructionist program is as an expression of restiveness under authority. The deconstructionist responds to some person or group claiming authority over him by attempting to expose its pronouncements as hopelessly ambiguous or conflicted. Hence law is said to be an inconsistent set of principles from which any conclusion a lawyer or judge wishes to draw can be derived. But this way of reading the deconstructionist program leads to paradox: if we know that some person or group has a claim to authority and that we have grounds to question or limit that authority, the apparent meaning of at least some of its pronouncements must already be known. And the mere fact of writing a book or article means that the problems of communication have been at least provisionally solved.

One route to the conclusions reached by deconstructionists involves the concept of translation.[6] If, as many philosophers now believe, our beliefs are tested holistically, there being no such thing as a crucial experiment, serious problems about meaning and translation immediately begin to arise. For, although strict verificationism is untenable, it is still hard to see how a word could be given a meaning apart from its connections with other members of the web of belief. If I claim to know the meaning of the word *gold*, but am unable either to identify samples of gold or to describe the implications of a given sample's being gold, it is hard to see what substance my claim will have. Hence we are threatened with *meaning holism*, according to which the meaning of a word or sentence depends upon its entire context in the culture in which it is uttered and the idiosyncratic character of the person who utters it.

Translation from one language to another will then be impossible, since each language will have its unique history and cultural geography, in which particular words and phrases would find their place. And the same would be true of communication between individuals, since each of us has an idiosyncratic personal history and a distinct family of needs and purposes. And if it is not possible for two people to understand the same sentence in the same way, the question of truth will not even arise.

Again: translation is contextual and pragmatic. Different principles are involved when we translate poetry, documents having religious authority, and scientific treatises. And all translation must take into account the differing cultural contexts in which the document translated and the intended audience exist. Hence meaning and consequently truth also are contextual and pragmatic and vulnerable to the diverging purposes of human beings. The alternative is to hold that translators should not even attempt to preserve the meaning of the texts they translate.

In order to prevent such conclusions, two things must be done. First, it is necessary to defend a moderate holism, according to which some parts of the web of belief are accorded a provisional independence of the rest and the same is done for the meaning of our words and sentences. But this sort of segmentation of belief is of necessity pragmatic and contextual, and hence subject to change as our needs and purposes change. Hence it is necessary, second, to hold, at least as a matter of rational faith, that the needs and purposes of human beings will continue to converge sufficiently to make discourse possible. And some power other than our own individual or collective efforts will be necessary in order to secure this result.

Deconstruction has had great impact on the intellectual life of the West, even in unlikely fields such as mathematics.[7] No longer do many thinkers look for "diamonds," that is, truths both informative and certain. Instead they tell "stories," of which they acknowledge themselves the creators. And there is, they say, nothing more to truth—even the truth of the story theory itself—than the stories human beings choose to tell. As a bumper sticker puts it, "I'VE GIVEN UP LOOKING FOR TRUTH, AND AM LOOKING FOR A GOOD FANTASY."

Let us set aside some of the claims that have been built into the "diamond theory," such as that human beings have discovered many diamonds or that the theorems of Euclidean mathematics are among them. As far as I can see, the diamond theory is consistent with considerable modesty about one's ability to discover diamonds. The issue is whether diamonds can be excluded a priori.

When we look again at the story conception of truth, two

points become evident. First, there are some stories, such as nazi racial ideology, that must be rejected, unless we are prepared to be nihilists in both the philosophical and the popular sense. Second, there are stories, such as the dialogues of Plato and the narratives of Biblical religion, that imply belief in a Truth independent of human purposes and conventions, though not one that is easy to obtain. (In the Biblical case the Truth cannot be obtained by human effort, but only by divine grace.)

Adherents of the story theory must therefore answer two questions: By what standard do they exclude the first sort of story, and by what right do they exclude the second? In the absence of answers to these questions, the story theory of truth can be set aside. At the same time there may be true stories, speeches and writings cast in narrative form that carry with them important Truths. The Biblical and Socratic stories are prima facie examples: if they can be made to cohere, their claim on our assent will be overwhelming.

Not everyone who practices deconstruction will accept a radical reading of the deconstructionist program. One advocate of deconstruction, for example, writes:

> It is not that identity is drowned in otherness, but that it is *necessarily* open to it, contaminated by it. . . . The value and necessity of pure concepts and categories are not denied, but they are no longer the last word. . . . Deconstruction is not a defense of formlessness, but a regulated overflowing of established boundaries.[8]

In a sentence, such a deconstructionist does not deny the existence of stable meanings but insists only that the surrounding context of "deviant" uses always stands ready to qualify the application of such meanings.

This reading of the deconstructionist program seems admirably commonsensical, until one presses the issue of how the regulations that are supposed to restrict the overflowing of established boundaries are to be established, interpreted, and enforced. Then it will be clear that the same skeptical arguments that can be employed against simpler forms of essentialism can be invoked against the attempts to limit permissible deviance. (At least it should be clear that the problem of interpreting deconstructionist texts is a real one.) Hence consideration of the nature and structure of our language leads quite directly to two central questions of social and political philosophy: whether the tendency toward chaos in our institutions and practices can be restrained except by authority and whether the claims of authority can be maintained except by force.

Let us therefore consider the connection many have seen between nihilism (and the particular form of nihilism called "deconstruction") and left-wing politics of a broadly anarchist sort. The key idea here is that, if one deconstructs the principles employed in institutional structures, the result will be a permanent revolution, both political and cultural, in which the terms of human association will be open to constant revision. (The deconstructionist had better not say that they will necessarily be negotiated anew on every occasion, since to do so would be to involve himself in the very essentialism he condemns.)

There is no logical reason why a nihilist should not adopt any principles he pleases on the experiential level. But, politically and rhetorically, advocates of change would be ill-advised to inscribe "DECONSTRUCTION" on their banners. For if their arguments for change are such as can be turned against any institution or practice, reform and revolution will alike be futile. And adherents of the status quo, if they are not utter idiots, can be depended on to point out this fact.

It is always possible to adopt radicalism as a personal stance, and with it whatever ideological framework seems pleasing at the time. This move is inconsistent with Marxism in any of its traditional forms, since both as theory and as practice Marxism rests on the belief that there is a movement of history from lower to higher stages that is a source of guidance in political action: a movement guaranteed by forces outside individuals and the norms and explicit purposes of their societies. Without this assumption, however, the rhetoric and concepts of

Marxism are available for use by any group you please. But it is absurd for such a group to appeal to supposedly neutral norms such as academic freedom and the First Amendment when some group whose interests or sensibilities it has been attacking decides to retaliate.

For deconstruction means the collapse of the critical level, so that when claims are in conflict there is no common standard to which the parties can appeal. Any purported adjudication merely takes sides or at best advocates a third factional view. And this is true, not merely of "fundamental" disputes, but of all disputes. I now consider one particular way nihilism at the critical level can seep down to the experiential level, or disturbances at the experiential level can affect the criterial level.

There is a profound experiential connection between nihilism and sexuality.[9] This connection is reflected in judgments many people find harsh and unbalanced, such as that, apart from excusing conditions, sexual sin is always mortal. In the eyes of many persons, sexual morality is crucial not only to morality but to an entire picture of the world, and the least laxity in this area is a threat to the entire structure. But the perceived connection between sex and nihilism is also reflected in the fact that other persons take as a central priority the legitimation of sexual practices hitherto denounced as abominations. Such persons accompany their efforts with an obscure sense that in attacking "society's" sexual morality they are struggling for a far wider and deeper liberation. My present purpose is to ask why there is so much emotional and ideological investment in a domain that could easily be regarded as peripheral.

I begin by noticing the enormous variety of perspectives human beings have taken on their sexuality. This variety is reflected, for example, in the broad range of sexual language: sexual acts are described as "lovemaking" and as "fucking" and as many other things.

At one end of the spectrum, human beings regard sex as the pleasurable release of emotional tension, accomplished through friction on the genital organs. Masturbation, on this view, is not merely a legitimate, but the paradigmatic, form of sexual experience—and desirable in that it avoids the emotional complications, and the risk of infection and pregnancy, that other forms of sexual experience entail. At the other end, procreative sexual intercourse is seen as a near-sacrament, since it enables us to cooperate with God in the creation of new life. Other forms of sexual expression are condemned as desecrations (as black masses are).

Most people have views somewhere between these extremes, often drawing on both in a not fully consistent fashion. But that a facet of human life in which everyone takes a spontaneous interest is capable of diverse interpretations goes a long way toward explaining the perceived connection between sex and nihilism. The intellectual, imaginative, and emotional edifices that human beings construct about their sexuality are peculiarly vulnerable to the assaults of deconstructionists, assaults in which intelligence and impulse are allies. Since most people interpret their sexual and other social experience in terms of gender difference, homosexuality and other forms of gender ambiguity have a special tendency to raise nihilistic spectres. But, in a different way, the possibility of mere sexual appetite, even directed solely at the members of the opposite sex, threatens to undercut the conceptions of love and fidelity that many people regard as central to their understanding of human sexual life. And if the structures of meaning that surround human sexuality are highly vulnerable, other structures may also turn out to be far less solid than they seem.

I would not have it thought, however, that sexual anarchy is the only, or even the most important, experiential source of nihilistic concerns. Reading student papers, for example, often raises the question of whether communication is possible across generational and cultural barriers.

THE DEATH OF GOD

The time has now come to connect the account of nihilism just given with nihilism as traditionally understood. I begin, as is customary, with Nietzsche's saying that God is dead.[10] Five features of this assertion deserve notice.

First, Nietzsche does not argue for the proposition that God is dead. Unlike atheists of another stripe, he presents no arguments (from evil, say) for the nonexistence of God. And by avoiding such arguments, he avoids also the theoretical commitments (say to a hierarchy of values independent of anyone's decision) they might entail. Perhaps he believes that science and technology have rendered God's existence incredible, but he makes no attempt to explain how or why this is so. He presumes that God's death is evident to anyone who confronts the issue honestly.

Second, he prefers the paradoxical (not to say melodramatic) formula "God is dead" to the tamer "There is no God." If anything is analytic of God as traditionally understood, it is that if He ever existed, He exists still. On some accounts the very existence of God is analytic, but the paradoxical character of a proclamation of His death is more manifest than that of an affirmation of His nonexistence.

Third, Nietzsche's saying is not directed against every form of religion. Ancient Greek religion and contemporary goddess spirituality can easily be interpreted as features of the self-understanding and self-assertion of certain groups, and their "gods" as frank projections of aspects of the personality of their worshippers. As such they escape Nietzsche's attack, since they make no claim to transcendence.

Fourth, his attack is not directed at Christianity (or monotheistic religion) alone. Nietzsche also rejects philosophies such as those of Plato and Kant (even in their nonreligious interpretations), and his position also requires the rejection of those forms of Marxism that suppose that history has a knowable structure that limits political possibility (and hence also legitimate political activity). These beliefs Nietzsche would regard as watered-down versions of belief in God.

Finally, Nietzsche considers his saying to be as subversive of intellectual life as traditionally conceived in the West as of religious belief. A remark of particular interest is the following: "I am afraid that we are not rid of God because we still have faith in grammar."¹¹ This rejection of the rationalistic tradition of the West provides a warrant for the melodrama of Nietzsche's formulations: it is nothing to *him* that "If there once was a God, there still is one" is analytic.

What these features of Nietzsche's proclamation show is that he is proposing or announcing a conceptual shift, which we may provisionally describe as one from theism (and Platonism) to naturalism. The line between proposing and announcing a conceptual shift is not clear: one way such shifts are brought about is by declaring that they have already taken place.¹² The effect of this shift is to require the abandonment of any belief in a standpoint external to the self-understanding and self-assertion of individuals and groups from which their conceptions of the world and their place in it can be evaluated. Science thus becomes nothing but the development of theories and techniques within the historically existing scientific community, as stimulated and constrained by the technological and military demands of advanced industrial societies.

By *naturalism* I mean more than a denial that the world is created by God, and less than a rigorous materialism. I mean the belief that rationality is exhausted in the adjustment of means to ends, and reality by those natural regularities means/ends rationality presupposes.¹³ I do not understand naturalism to require a strict determinism, so long as deviations are random and not large enough to disrupt means/ends rationality in a significant way.

Naturalists protect themselves against nihilism in two ways. The first is a belief that standards of rationality are unproblematic. It may be difficult to apply them to some cases, but it is never seriously in question what they are. The second is a belief that the ends of human life are adequately summed up in the word *happiness*. From these premises it follows that the rational pursuit of happiness provides a sufficient control on our reasoning to keep the threat of nihilism at bay. But naturalism also supports what may be called a "practices" view of knowledge and evaluation, a view that undercuts the defenses against nihilism that naturalists have constructed.

A practices view of knowledge and evaluation is required if

we are even going to try to do without supersensible essences and immanent forms. We must base our evaluations and claims to know on the bare fact that human beings prefer some things to others, make claims to know, and question one another's statements. In the course of so doing, we manage to apply the same word in novel contexts. As Wittgenstein would say, that is how the game is played.

Some practices contain norms regulating other practices and in this sense claim hegemony over them. Mathematics limits what can be said in physics, and physics provides the laws applied in engineering. What was called during the Watergate hearings "Politics with a capital P" controls the content and scope of law. And these hierarchies are sometimes reversed: physics is tested experimentally with the help of engineering; physics sets the agenda for creative mathematical work; the shared understandings that shape American politics are deeply legalistic. Again: that is the way the game is played.

But the practices view undercuts the defenses against nihilism that naturalists have erected. Scientific rationality is only one of many possible ways of investigating the world and moreover has a different meaning in different historical epochs. And happiness includes a variety of heterogeneous and incommensurable ends, which are ranked and weighted differently by different persons. When conflicts arise among different conceptions of the good, a practices view of knowledge and evaluation is left helpless. We are left with what may be called a "squawk box conception" of knowledge, according to which human beings say various things when subjected to various stimuli, and that is all there is to be said.

REPRESSING NIHILISM

Three possible responses to the threat of nihilism can be distinguished. One is the project of repressing nihilism, the second that of accepting nihilism, the third that of transcending nihilism. To repress nihilism is to avoid nihilistic conclusions by not asking the questions of justification that lead to nihilistic answers. (Compare the saying that civilization is the art of keeping things at bay.)

Naturalistic critics of the cosmological argument assert that it makes no sense to ask for an explanation of the sum of contingent things.[14] In the same way, those who repress nihilism argue that we should reject any question concerning the soundness of our practices. Given the tendency of human beings to press inquiries, this means one of two things.

Either it means seizing on some practice (say scientific investigation) and treating it as needing no external justification (and giving no justification, either, for the decision to treat this practice and not some other as sovereign). Or it means admitting a circle or infinite regress of justificatory practices. Neither strategy is satisfactory.

Adherents of the first strategy must deal with the fact that not everybody is prepared to accept their privileged practice and that, among those who do, not everybody is prepared to accord it sovereignty. Occultism, extreme political and social ideologies, countercultural movements, and sectarian religions have flourished under the supposed reign of scientific rationality. One imagines the adherent of scientific rationality sadly (or stridently) reiterating his commitments as the tides of unreason rise ever higher. Less colorfully, a practices view of knowledge and evaluation must acknowledge the facts discussed in this paragraph in its picture of our form of life.

More helpful is the attempt to avoid those questions that tend toward nihilism by allowing a circle or infinite regress of justificatory practices constituting a civilization (compare the section Third Interpretation: The Sovereignty of the Good, in chapter 3). No a priori limit will be placed on justificatory questions, but the kind of ultimate question that leads to nihilistic answers will be postponed indefinitely.

But people do question the credentials of entire civilizations: that, too, is how the language game is played. Nor can the defender of the project of repressing nihilism give any reason for refusing to examine these credentials. For such an answer would ascribe sovereignty to the standpoint from which this answer is given.

ACCEPTING NIHILISM

On the approach to philosophical issues taken here, accepting nihilism and proceeding with business as usual is one possible strategy. For our practices have an inertia that protects them from immediate destruction, even when one has yielded to metaphysical despair.

The acceptance of nihilism can take at least two forms. One—suggested by Kierkegaard's aesthetic mode—involves plunging into the practices in which one engages, enjoying them for their own sake, and deliberately refusing to look for the justification one knows is not forthcoming. But this approach simultaneously presupposes and repudiates a reflective attitude toward the practices in which one takes part.

The second way of accepting nihilism is suggested by some Eastern religion and Kierkegaard's "Religiousness A."[15] One accepts the fact that the practices in which one engages are pointless but persists in them so far (and only so far) as one's nature as a fleshy being requires it. The futility of human striving is a source of comfort when things go badly.

The issue for both this and all other ways of dealing with nihilism without confronting and transcending it is whether it can be accepted without a corrosive effect on our practices: it is whether nihilism can be contained. From a narrowly logical point of view there is no reason why accepted or repressed nihilism should affect our ordinary practices, so long as questions of justification are avoided.

But there are two objections to the project of containing nihilism. First, it means stopping requests for justification at a point conceded to be arbitrary or at best justified by the requirements of a particular inquiry. Questions that naturally arise when human beings inquire are rejected on no better grounds than that of our inability to answer them.

Second, many men and women believe that our practices are being corroded by nihilism. Much contemporary art, music, and literature can be interpreted as a warning of the impending disintegration of our civilization under the corrosive influence of a nihilism unsuccessfully contained. We are not required to accept this evidence at face value: perhaps the phenomena that traditionalists interpret as evidences of disintegration are in fact evidence not only of an end of an old world, but of the birth of a new. But the coming into being of a new world requires that some people believe in its organizing principles, and not merely acquiesce in the practices it involves. It requires that nihilism not be accepted and contained, but overcome.

TRANSCENDING NIHILISM

I now compare my argument with the contention, common among Evangelical writers, that nihilism, both intellectual and moral, results from the rejection of Biblical revelation under the corrosive impact of the naturalistic presuppositions of our culture (and in particular of Biblical criticism).[16] Skepticism about the miraculous is the most obvious manifestation of these presuppositions.

But not all Biblical difficulties result from naturalistic presuppositions. There are at least two kinds of Biblical difficulty that could not be resolved by postulating a miracle: moral difficulties, such as those concerning the extermination of the Canaanites, and problems of internal consistency, such as Psalm 51, ascribed to David, which presupposes the destruction of Jerusalem. Hence one cannot attribute all resistance to Biblical authority to the naturalistic presuppositions of modern readers. Nor can one expect to cure nihilism merely by insisting on Biblical revelation.

Still, a deistic or pantheistic perspective does not help much in overcoming nihilism. For such a perspective takes all phenomena, including our intellectual and other practices, as equally manifestations of God. Hence all ways of thinking, talking, and living will be equally divine, and hence no ranking of our various practices will be possible. Equally useless is a Manichean perspective, which regards our ordinary life as something from which we need to be saved. What is required is a perspective that makes it possible to rank human phenomena according to their differing relations to an absolute standpoint. In other words, we need some version of the traditional religions of the West, though *what* version my argument does not say. An explicit defense of a theistic resolution of our difficulties will be the concern of the next chapter.

In sum: this chapter has interpreted nihilism and considered some strategies for overcoming it. My understanding of nihilism has been shaped by what I have called the "practices view" of knowledge and evaluation, in which what is foundational are our various ways of dealing with our environment. Nihilism asserts that these practices are meaningless games that stand between us and the realization that our world is without sense. I have suggested that the only escape from nihilism is through the acceptance of a picture of the world as sustained by a God for Whom the course of the world, in all its detail, is not a matter of indifference.

6

GOD

IT IS NOW MY PURPOSE to articulate reasons that seem to me capable of convincing anyone for whom the question is an open one[1] that we are warranted in holding that there is a God, that is, a Being, at least legitimately thought of as a Person, Who is the source of all being and goodness and is thus capable of resolving our moral and epistemic conflicts (which is not the same as saying that He has in fact done so).[2] The strategy of my argument is to employ a version of the moral argument for the existence of God as a springboard from which to develop an analogous argument from the normative character of metaphysical and epistemological principles.

THE MORAL ARGUMENT

I begin with a version of the moral argument for the existence of God. Ethics does not merely designate some states of affairs as good or bad; it designates some actions as obligatory or forbidden. To some forms of human activity, which otherwise we might regard as less than ideal, it gives what the Irish nationalist Roger Casement called "an awful No." The interpretation of such imperatives is an important issue for ethical theory; religious believers characteristically understand them as the commands of God, an interpretation that affects the way they approach concrete moral issues. Some of the views considered in this book imply that this sense of categorical imperative should be abandoned, but for now I shall assume that it is to be retained.

I now argue that the theistic interpretation of moral imperatives, although not the only possible one (and in fact somewhat one-sided), is at least as attractive as any alternative. If God does not exist,[3] some other interpretation of moral imperatives will have to be found: most probably the interpretation will vary from moral requirement to moral requirement. (Compare chapter 4; also First Interpretation: A Relativism of Multiple Ends, in chapter 3.) But, if God does exist, it is plausible to interpret moral requirements as divine in origin. And the plausibility of theistic interpretation gives at least some reason for asserting that there is a God.

What is distinctive in theistic ethics arises from the belief that union or communion with God is the highest good for a human being. Making this claim the center of theistic ethics has a number of implications. Friendships, loves, and loyalties among human beings are at once sources of obligation, ways of coming to recognize obligations already present, and motives for doing what is right. The same may be said of a human being's relationship to God.

The good of God's friendship has a double aspect, as God is believed to be both the source of our existence and our Supreme Good. On the one hand, to stand in a proper relationship with God is to be at peace with oneself; one's relationship with God is in this respect parallel to, though more profound and intimate than, one's relationship with one's parents and one's country. On the other hand, union or communion with God can stand as our highest end—not as our only end, but as an end that, since it takes precedence over all others in cases of conflict, can establish an order among what would otherwise be a chaos of conflicting considerations. And since God is not only the Supreme Good but also the Creator of all lesser goods, the pursuit and enjoyment of such goods within the limits established by God can be brought into systematic harmony with the pursuit of a right relationship with God.

The most persistent objection to a theistic interpretation of moral imperatives is that it represents a version of the doctrine that might makes right: hence the notion that, for a theist, moral norms are orders backed with the threat of hellfire. The only possible answer is that power and goodness are not separable in God as in human beings. In the words of Peter Geach, "all the divine attributes, if thought out, coincide: God's power and knowledge and will and truth are all one."[4]

THE ARGUMENT CONTINUED

Other interpretations of moral imperatives run into difficulty. If moral requirements are self-imposed, it is hard to distinguish morality from inclination. Treating the demands of morality as universal does not help matters. If I dislike the practice of putting ice in beer, I could wish that no one ever put ice in beer; the wish is both costless and pointless. To link moral imperatives to questions of human importance is to raise the issue of who decides, and by what criterion, what matters are of human importance. Men and women disagree about the moral importance of sexual behavior, for example. Those who hold that people who insist on bizarre (or nonutilitarian) moral principles have failed to rise to the level of critical thinking raise the issue of why critical thinking is morally or otherwise important.[5]

And any stronger interpretation of morality as a system of universal imperatives, say one that requires that one do something to ensure that the requirements one adheres to are followed in practice, fails to cover all cases, for example, my belief that Nero did wrong in having his mother killed.

Another interpretation of moral imperatives treats them as expressing the will of society, as expressed through such institutions as blame and punishment. We call such a theory of the right "conventionalist" and formulate it as follows: *Actions are right or wrong as the relevant community approves or condemns them, having considered all the relevant facts and arguments.* What constitutes the relevant community and what the ethics of collective deliberation may be are for the moment at least open questions.

But the conventionalist interpretation of moral imperatives neglects two points at which appeal to the individual conscience is inescapable: where the voice of society is divided and when the individual, as has happened with persons conventionally regarded as very admirable, is moved to reject the dominant voice of society and to insist on moral standards of his own. (Admiration for Socrates is conventional within our society, though candor requires me to report that a minority of my students condemn him.) In both sorts of case it is possible to appeal to conventionally recognized standards in support of the individual's position, but the same standards can also be used to support the dominant view. And a changing society is at constant risk of dividing into a multitude of subsocieties and subsubsocieties, even apart from the divisions caused by such facts as social class. Hence to regard society as the author of morality is to face a grim choice between immobility and chaos.

Moral imperatives may also be thought of as immanent in the facts themselves. Since I do not believe in a metaphysical chasm between fact and value, I cannot exclude such a reading of moral imperatives as impossible. But although facts impose demands, these demands sometimes conflict, and the resolution of such conflicts requires a principle not similarly immanent in the facts. Life is to be preserved and pain eased, but the moral problem of euthanasia cannot be resolved without invoking some higher-order principle establishing a relationship between these requirements.

Some find in history a pattern so clear and persuasive that only one morality remains tenable when this pattern is seen. But anyone who retains the least moral sensitivity will sometimes find it necessary to affirm moral standards neglected by history, and there is no reason to believe that those of a future society are necessarily preferable to ours. Trotsky could consign his defeated opponents to the trash can of history, but when he himself was defeated and killed, different images came to the fore. Trotsky's widow said of her dead husband: "The arms fell just as the arms in Titian's 'Descent from the Cross.'"[6]

The concept of progress is valuable so long as it functions as an article of rational faith, leading us to look for possibilities for desirable change in the Soviet Union, for example, rather than dismissing entire societies as the incarnation of ahistorical evil.[7] But such an article of rational faith cannot provide us with any criterion for deciding what changes are in fact desirable. (We have no reason to believe, for example, that technological progress or its cultural effects are always good.) And, even as an article of rational faith, a theory of history as progressive requires some extrahistorical agency to secure its realization. No human individual or group capable of collective action has the power to give history a direction.

Another rival to theistic accounts of the nature of moral imperatives is the ideal observer theory: roughly, the belief that moral imperatives express what a perfect Being would approve or condemn if such a Being existed. The question here is the force of the counterfactual "would." It is hard to see how it could be causal, and if it is logical, the ideal observer theory reduces to some form of the view that moral imperatives are immanent in the natural or social facts.

Kant provides the nontheistic interpretation of moral imperatives most popular among philosophers, but he purchases ontological economy at the cost of logical oddity. His categorical imperative (that we should act only on those maxims that we are prepared to will as universal laws) is imposed by the agent upon himself, but in such a way that differences of temperament and social situation among agents do not produce a variety of codes. He views morality as a set of demands detached from any authority, hanging, as it were, in metaphysical midair. Insofar as he bases ethics on some aspect of human nature, such as autonomy or rationality, the problems of the naturalistic tradition recur, even apart from the special difficulties that arise from Kant's assigning the root of morality to the noumenal realm.

I cannot claim to have exhausted all possible nontheistic explanations of the binding force of moral imperatives. But I have said enough to place the burden on the atheist to develop a plausible account of ethics without God.

The theistic account of the binding force of ethical norms is thus the most plausible of those available. But this conclusion supposes that there is a God, or at least that the concept of God is coherent and intelligible. Doubt upon the latter score does not arise only from the application of external (say, positivistic) criteria, but also from within theism itself. For the whole thrust of theistic doctrine is so to stress the difference between God and other beings as to raise the issue of how God, if He exists, can be talked about by human beings at all. And all theists of whom I am aware eventually say things that at least sound very strange. If God exists, the peculiar character of religious language arises from the peculiar epistemic position of believers who must, in this life at least, approach the object of their belief, as St. Paul put it, through "a dim reflection in a mirror."

MORALITY AND RATIONALITY

The crucial objection to the moral argument is that morality must find its place in the world as it is and that, apart from a desire to make sense of morality, belief in God is irrational or at best groundless.[8] But, when one considers the normative character of epistemic principles, including those that determine what utterances are to be regarded as intelligible, the moral argument for the existence of God can be generalized to evade this problem. Although norms governing our beliefs are strictly speaking moral only under special circumstances, for example, when the interests of others are involved, still a quasi-moral condemnation of those who nurse irrational beliefs is implied in such expressions as "superstitious" or "flaky."

An example of a rationality norm held by nearly everyone is that one should accept the simplest hypothesis consistent with the evidence. But the interpretation and application of this norm vary from person to person and from group to group. An atheist will maintain that simplicity requires that agents outside the sequence of events governed by scientific laws be excluded; an agnostic will simply decline to assert the existence of such an agent; and a theist will maintain that simplicity either requires or permits us to assert God's existence.

Now consider a metaphysical and epistemological perspective that excludes the possibility of the existence of God. Adherents of that perspective may regard it as the merest common sense, derivable in unproblematic fashion from the natural sciences or from everyday experience. But in fact there is no experience without an a priori structure, and natural science and everyday experience exclude belief in God only when their a priori structures are so construed as to exclude it. The question has an irreducibly normative aspect: ought we to so construe the norms of rational belief as to exclude, permit, or require belief in a Creator?

With the question of rationality cast in this normative mold, we are entitled to ask, as with moral norms strictly speaking, What is the source of requirements that, expressly or by implication, condemn belief in God as irrational? To condemn this question as a pseudoquestion forbids a question that many human beings, not all of them professional philosophers, have asked.

For those who do not believe in God, the most plausible answer is that the norms of rational belief are taught and upheld by some individual or group, such as the scientific community, that has assumed that authority. This answer corresponds to the conventionalist understanding of ethical imperatives, considered previously. Although those who belong to an intellectual community that affirms the existence of God, and who thus reject the legislation of the Vienna Circle or other such groups, can be stigmatized as deviants or condemned as rebels, they cannot in any useful sense be regarded as intellectually wrong. A common rhetorical addition, that secularism is the wave of the future, does not help the atheist's case.

The strict atheistical position is not the conventionalist one just considered; it affirms the universality of rationality norms that exclude belief in God, for example, as an unnecessary hypothesis. But the source of such norms is as obscure as is God, and hence it is not plausible that the existence of such norms could be regarded as an intelligible possibility, and the existence of God not. Yet it is here that the consistent atheist—including the variety of atheist for whom *God* is a word without sense—must rest his case. There are norms even theists must accept that expressly or implicitly preclude belief in God, but the source of these norms cannot be explored.[9]

Those who believe that the canons of rational argument have probative force independent of any authority can take two different positions. One position refers to the role of these canons in conversation: sometimes, at least, appeal to them persuades. But one must distinguish rational persuasion from other, often more effective, controversial tactics, such as scandal about opponents, or use of professorial authority to intimidate, or blackmail. Another position claims that the canons of rational argument carry their normative power within themselves and need no further support. This move is plausible only insofar as the norm in question has not been seriously challenged and in particular fails when the canons of rational argument are used to dislodge deeply entrenched beliefs such as belief in God.

On the other side, theists appeal to an authority higher than themselves, that is, God, Who will judge between them and unbelievers. If they are right, they are right; if they are not right, they are not wrong either, except on standards that turn out to be as mysterious as their beliefs. Hence anyone for whom theism is a real possibility has every reason to believe in God.

IS IT GOD?

A key issue for any argument for the existence of God is what the attributes of the "God" Whose existence is said to be established by it are. Thus an advantage of St. Anselm's "ontological" argument is that there can be no serious doubt that, if sound, it establishes the existence of God, as understood by Christians and other believers. (This is not to say that it establishes an adequate basis for Christian or other theistic religious belief, or even that St. Anselm is entitled to assert, on his premises, that the concept of God even makes sense.[10])

The argument made here implies the omnipotence and omniscience of God. These amount to the same thing: that a given proposition is true is equivalent to its being certified as such by God, Who is the Source of all being and the Judge of all disputed questions. Likewise God is omnipotent and omniscient about questions of value. That a given state of affairs is good, or that a given act is right, and that it is commended by God are equivalent propositions. God's perfect goodness follows from these premises, unless one can give an account of moral weakness in the absence of temptation or of motiveless moral perversity.[11]

A range of complex issues is related to the relationship between a proposition p and the equivalent proposition that God chooses or believes that p. One is the question of human free choice: are there states of affairs, such as those involving decisions, that, though infallibly known, are not decreed by God? Another concerns the relationship between the proposition that a given action is right, or a given state of affairs good, and the (equivalent) proposition that God commends that state of affairs.

Attention must be given to the nature of the claim that, of two logically equivalent propositions, one is nonetheless prior, in a sense other than that human beings reason from one to the other. Theists will reason from the occurrence of an event, even one involving sin, to the conclusion that it was, in some sense, God's will that it should occur. But the doctrine that our sins were foreordained by God has been a source of much scandal. I am inclined to query the quasi-temporal relations suggested by such claims of priority and suggest that the truth of p and God's certification of that truth are not only logically equivalent but logically simultaneous. This suggestion may require some modification for free agency, but I cannot explore this possibility here.

In dealing with the issues of logical priority and logical simultaneity, we must be careful to distinguish them from the order in which a particular (or even a typical) reasoner will reach a given pair of conclusions: this order will vary with the circumstances of the person reasoning. And in dealing with a pair of logically equivalent propositions, there is no point in asking the truth of which is a necessary condition for the possibility of the other: the relationship is mutual. Accordingly it requires further reflection to understand the relationship of logical priority or simultaneity that may be held to exist between the propositions that p is true and that God chooses or believes that p.

Another way of looking at logical priority examines concepts rather than propositions. If the natural numbers are defined by repeated applications of the successor relation, then *zero* is prior to *one*, *one* to *two*, and so forth. If God is defined as among other things a morally perfect being, then the concept of moral perfection, and hence also moral goodness, is prior to that of God. But there is no particular reason to suppose that a family of concepts need be defined in any particular order, or that the most convenient order is necessarily the most intuitive. All the truth-functional connectives can be defined in terms of *not-both* and *neither-nor*, but it is not intuitively plausible that such concepts are logically prior to negation or implication. Probably the best solution is that logical priority, and hence also logical simultaneity, is dependent on context and in particular on the purposes for which the family of concepts in question is used.

Thus the label that might be attached to my position—a "divine command theory of ethics and epistemology"—does not fit well. Although moral and epistemic standards have their warrant from God, it does not follow that it is possible that, God so decreeing, it might be right to torture babies for our pleasure, or that, God so decreeing, self-contradictory propositions could be true. Still, the principles that exclude such possibilities do have their warrant from God.

The warrant from God that attaches to moral and epistemic norms can be considered from two points of view. From a religious point of view, adherence to such norms is an aspect of friendship with God. The pursuit of Truth is thus a religious exercise even when the subject is in no way theological. From God's point of view, it is an aspect of His creation of the universe. And God, in creating the universe, determines also what nonactual possibilities there are. As St. Thomas Aquinas puts it, Divine Providence arranges that what will come about necessarily will come about necessarily, and that what will come about contingently will come about contingently as well.[12]

Moral and epistemic norms have the appearance of commands insofar as they address human beings who would prefer not to observe them. But if we consider them from God's standpoint, they are neither independent of Him nor subject to His arbitrary will. What C. S. Lewis says of moral norms is true of epistemic norms as well: "God neither *obeys* nor *creates* the moral law."[13] In God there is no priority among wisdom, goodness, and power: God's perfection includes all these without differentiation, although human beings may for their purposes emphasize one of them rather than another. Likewise God is the Creator both of the structural features of our world and of the particular things within it, though in a somewhat different mode.

Another way of formulating this conclusion is as an answer to Lewis Carroll's question in "What the Tortoise Said to Achilles." What requires us to move from p and *if p then q* is often called "the hardness of the logical must." And the hardness of the logical must, I am suggesting, arises from God. Or more precisely it is God Who supplies the imperative quality of logical and epistemological imperatives and in so doing makes possible the distinction between truth and error.[14]

A further issue is whether my argument, even if sound, establishes the existence of a personal God at all, or rather only that of a Truth, both moral and metaphysical, transcending human purposes and conventions that it has been the concern of pragmatists to attack and Platonists to defend (see chapter 3). Friendship with God could be understood as knowledge of such Truth and life according to its requirements. The existence of such a Truth is an implication of my argument: God's version of the true and right is normative for human beings and can claim to provide a universally binding resolution of all disputes (though it does not follow that such Truth is easily accessible or that anyone has the right to claim that he has attained it for a range of controversial issues). The issue is what further content the concept of God, as I here understand it, has beyond this.

A partial answer is that the existence of a Truth transcending human purposes and conventions has a more than merely intellectual importance, at least for philosophers (see chapter 2). To be a philosopher rather than a lawyer is to be concerned not only with persuading others or even oneself but with reaching a Truth that, in principle at least, is independent of what any human being or group believes. At least as a regulative ideal, belief in such a Truth is essential to the activity of trying to discover arguments and doctrines that will commend the assent of rational people generally, as distinct from trying to persuade particular audiences at particular times and places. And something more than a regulative ideal may be necessary if the philosopher is going to persevere in his efforts despite the formidable obstacles, both moral and material, to his efforts.

Beyond this the issue is, in part, one of picture preference. I find the picture of a person whose determinations resolve questions of being and value more satisfactory than that of a Truth hanging in metaphysical midair; others will no doubt disagree. One source of my preference is my disbelief in a metaphysical chasm between fact and value. If one believes in Truth as physical fact onto which values must somehow be superimposed, it is easier to believe in a Truth independent of any mind (and not just of any finite mind) than if one regards cognition as in every respect evaluative. The argument offered here can be described as one from the normative character of rationality: because standards of truth and knowledge call upon us to hold beliefs that we might prefer to reject, or reject beliefs we might prefer to retain, it always makes sense to ask what stands behind such norms besides the desires and attitudes of their adherents and the power of professors over students.

Thomas V. Morris suggests a line of thought that, if accepted, would resolve the remaining ambiguity decisively in favor of theism.[15] Morris proposes that God creates abstract entities in such a way as to preserve both their necessity and their objectivity. And, in so doing, God is also responsible for the modal status or propositions, and hence for what is possible and what not, in a way that avoids Descartes's notorious doctrine that God can do the impossible. The attempt to fix on a sense of "possible" independent of God's creative activity, in terms of which He can be said to have the power to do what is impossible, is inherently absurd.

I notice, first, that we lack a human model for the creation of necessary entities. The creative discoveries that mathematicians report take place within a preexisting framework. And literary and artistic creation, which provides at least a rough model for God's creation, if anything supports Descartes, for a work of fiction can include inconsistencies.[16]

More troubling still is the following line of thought: If God is the Creator of abstract entities, then God is the Creator of His own nature, that is, of that array of properties that is essential to Him. But if God is the Source of modality, then His existence is necessary; otherwise all modalities would be contingently held. In other words, His nature is a sufficient condition of His existence. But to cause, by one's creative activity, the logically sufficient conditions of something's existence is to create that thing; for example, to create a bachelor is to create an unmarried person, and to create a daughter is to create a parent (though not necessarily the person who becomes a parent through one's action).[17] Hence it appears that God is His own Creator, which seems to imply that He arose out of nothing. The traditional language, whereby God is *causa sui* or *a se*, says everything necessary without undue paradox.[18]

To reach this conclusion, we should adopt as our premise not that God is the Creator of abstract entities, but that He is their cause, or else that they come from Him. And, although

God so conceived could still be the Creator of contingent things in the customary sense, as regards abstract entities, necessary truths, and at least some of the rules of morality He is closer to the One of the Neoplatonists that many contemporary theists would be comfortable with.[19]

In order to link the arguments of this chapter with more conventional epistemological concerns, one requires further assumptions along the following lines: that God acts reliably; that He has created us in such a way that we are capable of knowing the world He has created; that He has placed us in an environment such that, when our cognitive faculties operate normally, knowledge results; and that nothing has happened such as to spoil irrevocably our capacity to know—that however severe the noetic effects of sin, for example, they do not amount to total depravity.[20] (I am told that Calvin was not a believer in total depravity in this sense.)

The theistic epistemology just sketched has as its principal rival the approach, more popular among contemporary philosophers, that invokes evolution to guarantee that our cognitive faculties will operate well enough to make it possible to survive and reproduce. But the evolutionary approach to epistemology is open to some serious objections.

First, we have cognitive capacities that are useless in the struggle for existence, such as our capacity to know the truth of the propositions of higher mathematics. Even if such knowledge should have survival value, it is hard to see how it could have had it for the distant ancestors in whom the capacity for it first arose.

Second, the theory of evolution never explains how a given trait arose. At most it explains how organisms lacking that trait would be unable to survive to produce offspring. Thus it takes us no further in epistemology than the following commonsense point: that our continued existence makes it probable that our cognitive capacities are not too deeply out of harmony with their environment (assuming, of course, that we can trust them well enough to make this inference).

Third, the fact that evolution is a scientific theory places severe limits on the support it can give to epistemology. In particular, evolution cannot help us explain why we are entitled to expect natural events to display sufficient regularity to make scientific knowledge possible. The frankly a priori character of theistic epistemology is in this context an advantage.

Fourth, if our reliance on our cognitive faculties rests on their ability to help us survive and reproduce, then different ways of employing these faculties are to be assessed in terms of their contribution to our survival and reproduction. Hence those who control the circumstances in which we live will also determine the standards by which our cognitive performance is to be evaluated; in a sentence, might makes right (Second Interpretation: Might as Right, chapter 3). That the evolutionary process is slower in its operations than the social control exerted by social and political elites makes no difference in principle.

The most fundamental question is whether God will uphold or reject our purposes, hopes, and convictions, including the persons in whom these purposes, hopes, and convictions reside. Very little follows from my argument at this point. It is self-defeating to believe in an epistemology of total depravity, that is, that every human thought, including this one, is hopelessly removed from Truth. And it is within God's power to transform radically the conditions of human existence, so that the Truth now only dimly glimpsed by us will be someday more clearly known. But the question whether God will favor us in this way concerns the free actions of a transcendent Person, understandable by us only through imaginative representations. In other words, it is a matter outside the domain of philosophy, and within that of religion.

7

RELIGION

I NOW TURN TO THE question of religion, beginning with that of definition.

ON DEFINING *RELIGION*

It is now far too late to complain of persuasive definitions,[1] as if they constituted a species of intellectual sharp practice. A definition of *violence* that includes ad hominem arguments along with rape and arson, or a definition of *fanaticism* that includes Kantians as well as Nazis, can be censured for its attempt to win cheap and therefore spurious intellectual victories. But no nonpersuasive definition of an evaluatively charged expression is possible.[2]

In the first place, any definition of a term[3] already in use, however lexical its intentions, will reject some actual uses as erroneous or stretched while suggesting new uses. Where the term in question is evaluatively charged, such smoothing and generalization of actual use will have an evaluative dimension. To argue that some actions people have called "terrorism" do not deserve the name, or that other actions to which people have denied the name do deserve it, is to take a position with strong evaluative implications. To such a conclusion, not only conceptual but also normative, considerations are relevant.

Second, even those relatively neutral definitions C. L.

Stevenson calls "detached"[4] designate some objects (or classes of objects) as worthy of attention and, for that reason, imply a preference for one of many possible methods of inquiry. Nor is it possible to speak here only of mutually tolerant interests in knowledge. Projects of inquiry are parts of broader research programs, and these in turn are linked to wider social, political, and religious movements. And what is true of detached definitions is true, a fortiori, of what Stevenson calls "re-emphatic" definitions, that is, of those whose point it is to call attention to analogies and distinction. Such questions must be regarded as merely verbal, to be settled by majority vote or other authority, so that discussion of interesting substantive issues can proceed. For there have been times and places where it has been a matter of dispute, among otherwise reasonable people, whether Jews were human beings.

A value-free definition of *religion* is thus impossible. But the evaluations that shape definitions of *religion* are particularly complex. Sometimes *religion*—and even more so *theology*—is used in a derogatory sense, in polemics against Marxism, for example. At other times *religion* is a good word, used to protect deviants, such as Jehovah's Witnesses or conscientious objectors, against penalties. More subtly, we encounter the view that religion, although a good thing on the whole, is not to be taken altogether seriously. This view is frequently found even among those who habitually take part in religious observances. Some Christian theologians have attempted to evade this attitude by distinguishing (true) Christian faith from (human) religiousness, including cultural deformations of Christianity. But the analogies between every known form of Christianity and Buddhism, for example, are too clear to be evaded by this strategy.

Opportunities for special pleading abound here. Where, as in the United States, the law endeavors to protect religion from government as well as government from religion, the definition of *religion* is an especially sensitive issue. For shifting definitions of *religion* can be used to favor beliefs and practices with which one is in sympathy and to penalize those to which one is hostile.[5]

On no view is every form of religion desirable. And to characterize a belief or practice as religious makes an apt polemical point only when it calls attention to a failure of self-knowledge; otherwise a group can happily embrace a characterization of its beliefs and practices as "religious."

RELIGION DEFINED

Two patterns of definition might be attempted. One looks for necessary and sufficient conditions: for sets of properties possessed by all and only religions. A second abandons the search for necessary and sufficient conditions and looks instead for a set of religion-making conditions, establishing a family resemblance among the various phenomena called "religion."[6] Neither pattern of analysis is altogether satisfactory.

Anyone who can find a usable set of necessary and sufficient conditions distinguishing Homeric religion and the more austere forms of Buddhism from all nonreligious forms of belief and practice will have performed a remarkable feat. But merely to list religion-making characteristics is to leave the subject in as much chaos as one found it: unless we can say that the idea of salvation is more central to religion than the existence of sacred objects, little understanding of religion will be possible.

I take the standard forms of Christianity as my paradigm of religion, rather than Judaism or the movement headed by the Reverend Sun Myung Moon. A consequence of this decision is to make it more difficult (which is not to say impossible) to see religion primarily as a matter of communal affiliation, inherited or voluntary, without essential transcendent reference. My justification for so doing is in part autobiographical, but it gains significant support from ordinary language as well. Someone who takes part in Jewish cultural life without believing in the God of Israel is what most people call a nonreligious Jew. But the most important impulse behind my choice of paradigm is philosophical: a desire to have the resulting definition address the question of under what conditions transcendent Truth can be apprehended by human beings.

Two central criteria for the existence of a religion can be distinguished. Where both of these criteria are satisfied, as in the central forms of Christianity, we can confidently say that a religion is present. When only one criterion is present, whether we call the phenomenon a religion will depend on criteria of a less central sort. Where neither is present, the phenomenon will be labeled nonreligious.

The first criterion is doctrinal: a religion affirms the existence of one or more superhuman agents, on whose favor the welfare of human beings depends. I say *superhuman*, not *supernatural*, since not every culture distinguishes between nature and supernature, and some philosophers see the distinction as obsolete even in the West.

A consequence of this criterion is that some forms of belief in flying saucers are nearly religious. Extraterrestrials who are indifferent to human beings are no more suitable as objects of religious devotion than are the indifferent gods of Epicurean philosophy. But if someone believes that his well-being depends on maintaining the good will of superior beings inhabiting another planet, he has moved at least a substantial way toward making his belief into a religion.

The second criterion is psychosocial or functional. A religion by the second criterion unifies, through a system of imaginative representations, the framework by which an individual or group regulates its thought and life and thus manages to maintain in them some semblance of coherence. Many people will suppose that the second criterion is appropriate for the higher religions, whereas the first picks out a class of superstitions. And others will hold that the first criterion is necessary for the presence of a full-blooded religion, whereas the second alone picks out only watered-down modernistic "faiths." But—though the issues are not entirely separate—we are not here concerned with good versus bad religion, but with characteristics common to good and bad religions alike.

The two criteria are moreover connected in the following way: Suppose there is a superior Being on whom our welfare depends. We cannot expect to understand fully or adequately the purposes of such a Being, any more than our pets are able to understand our purposes. If the Being's purposes are wholly beyond our understanding, so much so that even with the Being's help we cannot hope to understand them at all, then there is nothing more to be said. But if partial and inadequate understanding of the Being's purposes is possible, we should expect the verbal formulae by which we express this understanding to strain at the limits of our language: in other words, to be imaginative representations of the sort marked out by the second criterion.

Religion is both an individual and a group phenomenon, comprising "faith" in an individual and "tradition" in a group.[7] An individual's faith is both stimulated and informed by the tradition he takes as normative, and one important expression of a faith is the transmission of the corresponding tradition (perhaps reformed) to others. Faiths that are sustained by, and help sustain, the Christian and Buddhist traditions have enough in common to be discussed together as examples of Christian and of Buddhist faith. This does not imply that Christians and Buddhists are primarily concerned with sustaining Christianity and Buddhism; on the contrary, the central concern of a devout Christian is God (or Christ) and that of a Buddhist, Nirvana.

Every individual and every group has a framework, an a priori: a set of presuppositions that make thought and life possible. It does not follow that every individual or group is religious, even by the second criterion, for a framework can lack unity of any sort and be a mere inherited conglomerate. Or the adherents of a framework may give it a unity by means of clear and distinct ideas rather than by means of imaginative representations. They may believe, in the somewhat ironic words of Wittgenstein, that "what can be said at all can be said clearly, and what we cannot talk about we must pass over in silence."[8]

By a representation is meant some form of nonliteral speech—say a paradox or a myth—whose point is to convey what cannot be expressed literally. A myth need not be historically false, but it dramatizes whatever historical truth it may contain in order to convey what its adherents believe is a non-historical truth. And for many myths the question of historicity does not arise, since they portray in narrative form what happens before or after history. A paradox, taken literally, is self-contradictory and hence false: it asserts, for example, that the same entity is at once unqualifiedly God and unqualifiedly human. But to take a paradox in this way is to miss its point, which is to direct the mind beyond what can be explained literally.[9]

Another reading of the concept of a paradox that amounts to the same thing is as follows: the Incarnation is a mystery, which cannot be understood by human beings, except in a strictly limited sense with the help of God's grace. Hence the propositions that express the doctrine are bound to look self-contradictory, though careful philosophical argument will always be able to prevent a decisive demonstration of their self-contradictory character. Since the self-consistent propositions that express the doctrine of the Incarnation are known—and known to be self-consistent—by God alone, this approach does not differ in practice from the one just considered. It is always possible to avoid flat-out self-contradiction by making distinctions; the way these distinctions make a difference is not, on the view being considered, humanly knowable.[10]

Other forms of nonliteral speech employed in religious discourse include parables (which, unlike myths, do not even look like history), metaphors, action symbols, and, most austerely, statements in which words like *good* are projected by analogy to a Subject to which they do not ordinarily apply. That even analogy is a mode of nonliteral speech entails that theology cannot be a deductive discipline.[11]

In speaking in this way of nonliteral modes of speech, I open myself to the following objection: Literal speech is a philosopher's fiction: all speech involves the extension of the use of the words into a context in some respects novel. And the open texture of our concepts means that not only theology, but all reasoning, even in mathematics, is necessarily nondeductive (see Deconstruction, Politics, and Sex, chapter 5). We may grant that literalness is a matter of degree: to speak, for example, of an argument, an economy, and a person's health as sound involves a kind of metaphor or extended use. But the difference between such statements and calling Jesus "the Lamb of God" should be obvious to a reasonable observer. The continuities between religious and secular language are no threat to anything I want to say.

The imaginative representations used in religion differ from those involved in popular science, for example, in that they are, or are believed to be, irreducible. But those who employ representations are not infallible about their character. Such persons may be unaware of the pictorial character of their speech: such is probably the case of the simplest believers. They may resist the recognition that their speech is pictorial; if so, we may call them "fundamentalists," without troubling ourselves about whether those usually called "fundamentalists", are fundamentalists by this definition.[12] They may believe that their representations are irreducible, whereas in fact they can be translated without remainder into nonreligious terms; such is probably the case with some modernists, who unwittingly have reduced their faith to a political or therapeutic program. Finally, representations intended as merely rhetorical may escape the control of the underlying literal sense: parables designed to evade censorship may take on a life of their own and convey meanings far richer than those of mere political statement.[13]

Religious representations differ from those involved in ordinary poetry in that they attempt to unify a framework by which an individual or group conducts its thought and life. Such unity is achieved in one or both of two ways. It can be achieved in the ways a work of music, art, or literature is unified, that is, through a narrative structure, recurrent themes or images, and other devices of the same sort. It can also be achieved by directing those who adhere to a religion to a Supreme Good to which the beliefs and practices characteristic of the religion point.

These two modes of unification are connected, insofar as

the Supreme Good, toward which the beliefs and practices characteristic of a religion point, is that which cannot be expressed by ordinary prose but requires the methods of communication characteristic of religious discourse. And insofar as one version of the Supreme Good is union or communion with a Supreme Being, on Whose favor the welfare of human beings depends, religion by the second criterion can once again be linked to religion by the first.

We have now made contact with the tradition for which religion is a matter of a person's ultimate concern, but a definition in such terms fails to include the religion of Homeric Greece. Hence I employ reference to a Supreme Good as part of one criterion tending to establish the presence of a religion, rather than as a necessary or a sufficient condition for its existence. Nonetheless, the notion of a Supreme Good has a more central role than its place in my definitional structure would seem to indicate. For it is the Supreme Good that links the two criteria in a religion such as Christianity: it is the possibility of union or communion with God that provides a source of unity in the lives of believers, and to which the representations enacted in Christian practice point. And the Truth with which the Platonist in epistemology is concerned is nothing other than this Supreme Good in its cognitive aspect (see chapter 6).

Sometimes a group or individual will adopt two religions—in traditional China, Confucianism and Taoism; in Japan, Buddhism and Shinto—each of which deals with the aspects of life the other neglects. In such cases, it is worthwhile to explore the possibility that the two traditions may form a compound—say Confucianism-Taoism—capable of being unified in the manner characteristic of religion, if only a suitable prophet or theologian arises.

It is now time to consider the relationship between the two criteria just expounded and less central criteria, such as the presence of a concept of salvation and the existence of sacred objects. Sacred objects are those that figure in the action symbols a religion includes. Salvation is release from the bondage that is the ordinary lot of human beings and participation in the better world religious representations portray, including participation in the Supreme Good that provides believers with their principle of unity.

Other less central criteria include the existence of an organized community, of a canon of Scripture, of practices such as prayer, and of a characteristic strategy for dealing with those crises that threaten to disrupt the life of an individual or group: maturation, sexuality, child rearing, moral conflict (including guilt), suffering, and especially death. We also expect a religion to embody a protest against those aspects of the existing order that keep human beings in bondage, though not to preach rebellion in the most thoroughgoing sense.

Prayer is a natural way of dealing with a superior Being, on whose favor we depend. As for organized communities, canons of Scripture, and the like, if a set of representations is to be maintained and transmitted to the next generation, there will have to be some regular provision for doing so. (The very existence of religious representations, like any other form of language, requires community support, but not formal organization as such.) Appeal to a Supreme Good, and to that which gives unity to the life of an individual or group, is particularly likely in times of personal and social crisis, when it becomes apparent that (in the words of the Book of Common Prayer) "we have no power of ourselves to help ourselves."[14] And one thing that is hoped for from superior beings is that they should rescue those undergoing crisis or disfavored by the normal workings of their society.[15]

RELIGIOUS TRUTH

Some Medieval sectarians held that Judas Iscariot was the Messiah, on the ground that his betrayal of Jesus was necessary to our salvation.[16] On its face, this doctrine violates two basic principles of the Christian faith: (1) Jesus, and Jesus alone, is the Messiah. (2) Our salvation is attained by good works, not by evil acts such as the betrayal of a friend.

But neither of these considerations is as decisive as it looks. (1) How there can be two Messiahs, and yet only one, is admittedly a mystery. But arithmetical mysteries are not as such unacceptable to Christians. And (2) (a) it must be shown that the betrayal of a friend is without exception wrong; an initially plausible exception is when that betrayal would accomplish the salvation of the world. (b) In any event it is not clear that our salvation cannot depend on wicked acts, for example, the ministrations of a wicked priest.

I am not arguing that Judas was the Messiah; the doctrine seems to me quite repulsive. But that even so repulsive a doctrine can receive a sophistical defense raises quite sharply the issue of the canons of theological reasoning, and less directly that of religious truth.

Religious doctrines concern realities that transcend ordinary experience; hence they are expressed in language that strains against the limits of what is ordinarily sayable. Religion therefore essentially involves metaphors, paradoxes, strained analogies, symbolic actions, and the like. Hence there arise two issues: what does it mean for a religious proposition to be true, and how does one decide what inferences among such propositions are valid?

A quick answer to the first question is that religious propositions are true if and only if they portray their Subject (God, or the Religious Reality) accurately. But a correspondence theory of truth is open to special objections in a religious context: since God by common consent transcends ordinary experience, there are special obstacles to comparing God talk to its object. I shall therefore concentrate here on the criteria by which a rational person would decide among rival claims to religious truth. The question of religious truth and that of the canons of theological reasoning thus turn out to be very closely connected.

There are some propositions belonging to religious systems that are also historical in a straightforward way. That Jesus, in the words of the Apostles' Creed, "was crucified, died, and was buried" are historical propositions in the fullest sense: if it makes a difference, they do not even involve miracles. Yet they are of central importance to the Christian faith. Hence Christianity at least is open to historical falsification.[17] But the theological importance of these historical facts lies within what cannot be expressed in ordinary prose. Let us call this realm the *numinous*.

Within the realm of the numinous, words depart from their ordinary senses, and thus ordinary principles of logic do not necessarily apply. All one can say is that an adequate account of religious doctrines and of theological logic must steer among three disastrous possibilities.

The first of these is *glossolalia*, or the formulation of religious doctrines in strictly unintelligible terms.[18] Barely concealed glossolalia takes place whenever it is held to be a matter of indifference what formularies one uses—whether one holds that God loves or hates us, for example—so long as one's heart is in the right place, one belongs to the right religious community, or whatever.

The second is *instrumentalism* (see chapter 3), by which I mean the judging of religious doctrines solely in terms of their this-worldly (political or psychological) effects. Effects such as salvation lie within the realm of the numinous, and hence the meaning of talk about them is here in question. Instrumentalism wholly subordinates the religious to the nonreligious and thus fails as an account of the meaning of religious doctrines.

The third is *fundamentalism*, which I use in an extended sense to include uncritical reliance on non-Scriptural authorities. If the citation of an authority in ordinary print fails to silence the doubter, perhaps citations in boldface will succeed. Fundamentalists ignore the need to invoke natural reason to recognize, interpret, and apply religious teachings: without a control of this sort we are left at the mercy of charismatic figures, however dubious; of ecclesiastical bureaucracies, however corrupt; and of ingenious interpretations, however sophistical.

To each of these errors there corresponds a necessary feature of religious thought. To glossolalia there corresponds the extraordinary character of religious discourse, from which the present discussion takes its start. To instrumentalism there corresponds the legitimate pragmatism of much religious thought: religious doctrines and practices are often judged by their fruits. (One must first ask whether a religious doctrine or practice produces the fruits its adherents promise. But the worth of these fruits is at least sometimes open to external evaluation: Jim Jones's doctrines are not vindicated because his followers were prepared to kill themselves and their children.) And to fundamentalism there corresponds the necessary positivity of religious doctrines and practices: Christians use bread and wine in the Eucharist, rather than rice and tea or pretzels and beer, because Jesus did.

In addition to the features of religious belief just cited, the following are of importance:

First, a person's religious beliefs are importantly a function of his background and experience, including the individuals and groups with whom he has come into contact. The same is true of political ideology, but not, at least not in the same way, of geographical beliefs, such as that Cuba is an island.

Second, there is no reason to reject as irrational ordinary people's ordinary reasons for accepting the religions they accept. If one believes that God is active in His creation, these ordinary reasons can be seen as His ordinary way of leading us to Him.

Third, formal doctrines and rules of conduct are often less important than the social and ritual atmosphere a given religious community projects and the (often complex) relationship between religion and daily life. The characters and personalities of the members of a religious group, and the rituals by which they celebrate their shared beliefs, reflect their worldview and for that reason are taken seriously in making religious decisions. Formal doctrine has a different role, in the attempts of leaders and other members of the community deliberately to shape its life.

Fourth, small matters are often religiously crucial. Jane may find the asymmetrical arrangement of candles on the altar of a sectarian religious group disturbing. Robert may find the passing out of evaluation forms after Mass tacky. Both are entitled to take these responses into account in judging religious issues.

Fifth, accepting a religious tradition is, in the first instance at least, accepting a certain picture of the world and its associated practices as a whole. A person accepts Christ as presented in a certain way, and with this acceptance comes the acceptances of the doctrines, practices, and moral code of a certain religious community. Questions of interpretation may arise later on, but in the first instance one accepts a religion as a whole.

But, sixth, not all religious controversies, or even all important ones, are reflected in denominational boundaries, or even the boundaries between major religions, both of which tend to reflect the controversies of the past. A Christian and a Buddhist may have more in common than two Christians.

Finally, there is an important source of instability in all religious systems that no institutional or doctrinal system is entirely able to contain. Not only are religious individuals and groups charged with continuing a complex tradition in novel historical and cultural contexts; the Power with which they are concerned retains the initiative and may demand a reshaping of the ways in which He is worshipped. Disputes between modernists and traditionalists are therefore to be expected.

These considerations form a background against which it is possible to assert two principles.[19] The first is a principle of immanence, according to which religion cannot wholly reject the world and its practices; the second is a principle of transcendence, according to which religion cannot identify itself wholly with the world or some portion of it, but must always stand in judgment on all our practices (including our religious practices).

The denial of immanence may be called *Manicheanism*. It involves some version of the doctrine of total depravity—either denying the possibility of living a good life or knowing truth in the world or denying any connection between our attempt to live well and know truth in the world and our salvation. Since such a doctrine requires us indiscriminately to reject all of our presuppositions and denies any credibility to our experiences, it deprives us of any possible reason for believing it to be true.[20] To the principle of immanence there corresponds an important spiritual principle, which may be called *Jonah's principle:* that God may condemn harshly, but never, in this life at least, irrevocably; that any voice that condemns us or others totally, and extends no hope of eventual salvation, does not come from Him. Doctrines and practices that violate immanence by requiring us too sharply to reject our spontaneous understanding of ourselves and our world—say the doctrine of infant damnation or the asserted power of the Pope to depose civil rulers—usually are quietly shelved, as members of the religious group in which they are held find it harder and harder to take them seriously.

The denial of transcendence may be called *reductionism.* Essentially, what the reductionist says is that the world (or some portion of it, such as the culture of Latin American revolutionaries) is acceptable as it is and that there is no need for religion. To the principle of transcendence corresponds *Jeremiah's principle,* that a voice that confirms us in our complacency is not from God either. (This includes not merely the complacency of the rich and powerful, but also that of those, however lowly their present condition, who are persuaded that they are the vanguard of history.) Doctrines that violate transcendence, such as the uncritical acceptance of prevailing moral and economic notions by religious teachers, may require formal repudiation by a religious community concerned to protect its own vitality.

I conclude this section with some advice to religious communities threatened with schism, as so many are these days. Such schisms characteristically arise from the interaction between a religious tradition and its cultural environment—often characterized as a conflict between the claims of tradition and the needs of the age. And it is the controversies attending such schisms that most sharply pose the issue of the nature of religious truth.

We begin by noticing that both terms of the conflict are

more complex than they appear. What the age wants is not necessarily what the age needs. To say that the age needs Truth, and that the Church has it, is too facile, since the nature of religious truth is at issue. Still, there is no virtue in telling people what they want to hear and calling the practice compassion: such a strategy promotes neither Truth, nor human happiness, nor the respect of one's audience. Moreover, dissatisfaction with modernity is one of the characteristic features of the modern experience: the only argument for deference to modern culture is that the modern world is the only one in which we can live.

On the other hand, there are deep ambiguities and conflicts within our religious traditions: problems of interpretation and application of religious ideas cannot be wholly blamed on the modern world. The tension between love and law is, for example, integral to Christianity, in the New Testament as much as anywhere.

Second, there are reasons, not only of peace but of truth, why open breaks within religious communities should be prevented if at all possible. One attractive feature of a large religious group is that it brings together persons of a wide variety of temperaments, cultural and class backgrounds, and so forth, and thus helps eliminate the biases that a narrow social base engenders. Those who claim to speak for God and those who (equally imperiously) claim to speak for the modern world need therefore pay careful heed to Cromwell's advice to consider the possibility that they are mistaken. Those whom one most dislikes, and whose departure from the group one might be most prepared to welcome, may be in possession of truths to which one might well pay heed.

So far a standard liberal argument. But the argument has a spiritual dimension that may be unnoticed by those who encounter it primarily in a secular context. God radically transcends the doctrines and practices by which human beings attempt to capture His presence. And therefore it is incumbent upon religious persons not to be too doctrinaire in their formulations.

But some religious communities claim to have in their possession infallible teaching authorities. The value of such authorities, should they exist, is clear: they impose some control on the tendency of human thought to generate an endless variety of positions and thus help maintain unity within the community. And this unity, I have just argued, is a means to Truth and not merely to peace.

But disputes concerning the reading of such authorities arise. Some find an infallible teaching in every possible case; others prefer to resolve doubtful cases in favor of freedom of inquiry. A special case of this dispute concerns the reading of documents agreed to contain infallible teachings: whether they are to be read in their maximum or their minimum sense. Similar problems arise for documents believed to possess not infallibility, but some lesser but still significant degree of authority.

A start toward resolution of this dispute is to require each party to adopt a stance of principled consistency with respect to the claims of authority. Liberal Catholics should ask themselves how much laxity they are prepared to tolerate with respect to Vatican II's condemnation of theological anti-Semitism; conservative Catholics how rigorously they are prepared to demand adherence to the social encyclicals. But disputes are likely to persist even when people adopt consistent principles, and not only because (as is notorious) it is possible to take virtually any position consistently if one is devious or perverse enough.

The argument of this section supports a minimizing approach to the claims of authority, though not one that is so minimizing as to garble the relevant texts. The same considerations of prudence and of respect for the divine Majesty that dictate hesitation in closing off discussion also dictate hesitation in giving a broad construction to the conclusive pronouncements admitted in one's tradition.

Here someone will object that I am infringing upon the Majesty of God, by denying Him the power to speak decisively within His world. But the issue is not what God can do, but what God has done, and this is one about which we must needs use our reason. And reason, although it does not exclude the possibility of infallible human authority,[21] gives us every ground to hesitate before accepting claims of infallibility in practice.

And appeals to tolerance such as made here are subject to important limitations. Never to act—never even to speak strongly—against those whose words or actions are injurious or offensive to those whose welfare one is bound to further is nothing more than spinelessness. There comes a point where tolerance and moderation leave one at the mercy of the intolerant and the immoderate. And attempts to state the limits of tolerance in statutelike terms fail: Mill's attempt to do so is irrelevant where what is at stake is the welfare of a moral and spiritual community. One is left in the end with the necessary, though the very ambiguous, virtue of prudence.

CONCLUSION

Until recently it was the custom in Italian universities for academics to declare their allegiance by the decorations above their desk: a crucifix or a portrait of Galileo. One of the tasks of this book has been to inquire whether both allegiances cannot be combined, despite the many forces that would oppose such a course. These include a contempt for spiritual concerns among worldly intellectuals and a retreat to glossolalia and mere authority among believers. Worst of all is a hostility to any sort of structure—moral, intellectual, or spiritual. Such a hostility may invoke critical intelligence along the way but in the end destroys such intelligence along with the practices and beliefs it criticizes.

I have here said what I have to say about the theoretical underpinnings of an attempt to combine the life of faith and the life of reason. The problems that arise when one attempts to embody this project in our world will be the concern, perhaps, of another volume.

NOTES

1. INTRODUCTION

1. *The Closing of the American Mind* (New York: Simon and Schuster, 1987), 25, 26. Bloom's point remains a good one, though he himself is not quite what he pretends to be; see my article "Allan Bloom: Nihilistic Conservative," *New Oxford Review* 55 (October 1988), 4-9.

2. Such views are frequently attributed to Derrida and Foucault, but I do not attempt a textual interpretation here; deconstruction as a program will be further considered in chapter 5.

3. The difference between *critical* and *criterial* is one of emphasis only. To speak of a critical standard emphasizes the role of such standards in challenging assertions; to speak of a criterial standard emphasizes its role in warranting assertions. But critical (criterial) statements usually play both roles.

4. *ESP and Parapsychology* (Buffalo, N.Y.: Prometheus, 1980), 307.

5. Hansel (ibid.) concedes this point.

6. George Price, "Science and the Supernatural," reprinted in *Philosophers in Wonderland*, ed. Peter A. French (Saint Paul: Llewellyn, 1975), 358. Price recanted in a postscript written for this anthology (p. 373).

7. The resurrected Jesus appeared only to his disciples and to St. Paul, who had persecuted the nascent Christian movement. St. Thomas the Apostle is reported to have proposed an empirical test but ultimately believed although that test was not performed (John 20:25, 27-28). Hence the Resurrection of Jesus lies outside the scope of secular history. But only on further metaphysical assumptions does

it follow that it did not take place. Many theological problems would have been avoided if this last distinction had been observed; see the section Religion Defined in chapter 7.

2. THE PUBLIC RESPONSIBILITIES OF PHILOSOPHERS

1. I prefer the Roman Catholic expression "special ethics," since it avoids the suggestion that discussions of ethical theory are mere intellectual exercises without practical importance.

2. Robert J. Rafalko, Tenth Congressional District, Pennsylvania, 1982. Jeff Orrenstein, Sixteenth District, Ohio, 1982.

3. See my *The Ethics of Homicide* (Ithaca, N.Y.: Cornell University Press, 1978; paperback forthcoming from Notre Dame Press.

4. This claim is common to ideologues of all persuasions. Compare Leszek Kolakowski, "The Conspiracy of the Ivory Tower Intellectuals," in *Essential Works of Marxism*, ed. Arthur P. Mendel (New York: Bantam, 1965), 347–70.

5. See Anthony Kenny ed., *Aquinas* (Garden City, N.Y.: Doubleday Anchor, 1969), 1–3.

6. For example, the assumption that it is the duty of a citizen to believe that whatever those in charge of his government say makes at least minimal sense, even if it would be instantly rejected as nonsense if anyone but a political leader said it.

7. This is the place to notice, however briefly, the "better red than dead" argument and its converse. Since free institutions would no more survive nuclear holocaust than they would Soviet conquest, and since a Communist-dominated world might still suffer nuclear war among rival factions, such arguments should be reformulated in terms of risk assessment in order to be taken seriously. It is also necessary to consider another argument against nuclear deterrence, less open to prudential considerations: that the intention to kill innocent people is immoral as such.

8. In fact Rorty attempts to turn this question into that of the value of particular writers, standing in a loose family relationship to one another and to Plato. "What are Philosophers For?" *Center Magazine* 16 (September–October 1983), 40–51. But he fails to address the issue, why the discussions begun by Socrates and Plato were worth beginning or are worth continuing.

9. "The Responsibility of Intellectuals," in *The Dissenting Academy*, ed. Theodore Roszak (New York: Pantheon Books, 1968), 256.

It is remarkable how little this article, read in retrospect, tells us about the responsibilities of intellectuals.

3. PRAGMATISM

1. On the traditional sense of *pragmatism*, see Gertrude Ezorsky, "Pragmatic Theory of Truth," and H. S. Thayer, "Pragmatism," in *Encyclopedia of Philosophy*, ed. Paul Edwards (New York: Macmillan, 1967), vol. 6, 426–36.
2. *Pragmatism* (Cleveland: Meridian, 1955), 196.
3. Citations in the text are to *Consequences of Pragmatism* (Minneapolis: University of Minnesota Press, 1982).
4. See also his *Philosophy and the Mirror of Nature* (Princeton: Princeton University Press, 1980), esp. pt. 4.
5. The phrase about correct rituals is of course a slander on objectivism of any plausible sort.
6. This passage reveals a fatal ambiguity in Rorty's approach to religion. On the one hand, he needs the premise that religion has been decisively superseded in order to lend plausibility to the conclusion that philosophy might suffer a similar fate. On the other hand, it is hard to see how religion—or anything—could be decisively superseded on Rorty's premises.
7. Henry F. May quotes John Dewey as writing: "The very existence of the social medium in which an individual lives, moves, and has his being is the standing effective agency of directing his activity." And he comments: "Only recently have we learned to fear, more than the old-fashioned visible tyrant, the pressures against which it is unthinkable to rebel." *The End of American Innocence* (Oxford: Oxford University Press, 1979), 152, citing John Dewey, *Democracy and Education* (New York: Macmillan, 1923), 33.

4. RELATIVISM

1. Examples include "hierarchy of values," "commitment," "absolute presupposition" (Collingwood); "language game" or "form of life" (Wittgenstein); "paradigm," "disciplinary matrix," or "core" (Kuhn); "blik" (Hare); "research program" (Lakatos); "conceptual scheme" (Strawson); "perspective," "vision," "faith," "dogma," "ideology," "myth," "tradition," and "worldview." "Dogma," "ideology," and "myth" are not here used in a derogatory sense.

2. See, for example, *Serbian Eastern Orthodox Diocese* v. *Milvojevich*, 96 S. Ct. 2372 (1976).

3. Cf. Herbert L. Hart, *The Concept of Law* (Oxford: Oxford University Press, 1972), chap. 6, sec. 2.

4. Cf. Richard H. Popkin, *The History of Scepticism from Erasmus to Spinoza* (Berkeley: University of California Press, 1979), esp. chap. 1.

5. Lawrie Resneck, "A Note on Relativism," *Philosophical Papers* 8 (1979), 69–71; and B. C. Postow, "Dishonest Relativism," *Analysis* 29 (1979), 45–48.

6. I here do not follow the version of relativism defended by Joseph Margolis; see his debate with Michael Wreen, *Philosophy and Phenomenological Research* 83 (1982), 83–97. The version of relativism expounded here does not involve any abandonment of the concept of truth.

7. Cf. Israel Scheffler, *Science and Subjectivity* (Indianapolis: Bobbs-Merrill, 1967), 1.

8. Collapse of relativism into subjectivism of a thoroughly nihilist sort is illustrated in Paul Feyerabend, *Against Method* (Atlantic Highlands, N.J.: Humanities Press, 1975). Feyerabend backtracks a bit in his *Science in a Free Society* (New York: Schocken, 1979).

9. The term *directly* is intended to avoid begging the question against those who believe they have a general theory of all possible frameworks such that they can establish incoherence of all but one.

10. The leaky boat argument is due to the historian J. H. Hexter.

11. See, for example, Donald Davidson, "On the Very Idea of a Conceptual Scheme," *Proceedings and Addresses of the American Philosophical Association* 42 (1973–74), 5–20.

12. Fred I. Dretske, *Seeing and Knowing* (Chicago: University of Chicago Press, 1969).

13. Those sympathetic to the drug culture should substitute another example: say, subjection to the sort of mind control said to be characteristic of cults.

14. I am here responding to arguments made by Margolis in conversation.

5. NIHILISM

1. For example, Hubert Dreyfus and Jane Rubin, "You Can't Get Something for Nothing," *Inquiry* 30 (1987), 33–75. For a useful,

though somewhat superficial, survey, see James W. Sire, *The Universe Next Door* (Downers Grove, Ill.: Intervarsity Press, 1976), chap. 5.

2. "What can be smashed should be smashed; what will stand the blow is good; what will fly into smithereens is rubbish." Dmitri Pisarev, quoted in Robert G. Olson, "Nihilism," *The Encyclopedia of Philosophy*, ed. Paul Edwards (New York: Macmillan, 1967), vol. 5, 515.

3. The view set forth in the text is an ideal type, but views like it are held by Ronald Dworkin, Bruce Ackerman, and John Rawls, though not by those liberals who rest their arguments on the high value of human autonomy, such as John Stuart Mill or Charles Fried. Even less open to charges of nihilism are those liberals for whom free inquiry is useful as a means to discovering the good life, for example, Mill and (in the contemporary debate) Will Kynlicka, "Liberalism and Communitarianism," *Canadian Journal of Philosophy* 18 (1988), 181–204.

4. "Twilight of the Idols," *The Portable Nietzsche* (New York: Viking, 1967), 486.

5. Ibid., "The Antichrist," sec. 26, 398.

6. My argument here is indebted to a debate between Hilary Putnam and Jerry Fodor at MIT, December 1987.

7. See the lucid exposition in Richard J. Trudeau, *The Non-Euclidean Revolution* (Boston: Birkhauser, 1986), chaps. 3 and 8.

8. Henry Staten, *Wittgenstein and Derrida* (Lincoln: University of Nebraska Press, 1984), 18, 19, 24.

9. An adequate treatment of the points sketched here would have to respond to the very rich discussion in Roger Scruton, *Sexual Desire* (New York: Free Press, 1986).

10. I do not here attempt a full-fledged interpretation of Nietzsche. If he tries to get beyond the nihilism of some of his utterances, it is still worthwhile to ponder them in their own right, since they have had considerable influence.

11. Nietzsche, "Twilight of the Idols," 483.

12. Compare Katharyn Pyne Parsons, "Nietzsche and Moral Change," *Nietzsche*, ed. Robert Solomon (Garden City, N.Y.: Anchor Books, 1973), chap. 9.

13. For a clear and frank statement, see Sidney Hook, "Naturalism and First Principles," *Philosophy of Religion*, ed. Steven M. Cahn (New York: Harper & Row, 1970), 335–60.

14. See Paul Edwards, "The Cosmological Argument," in *The Cos-*

mological Arguments, ed. Donald Burrill (Garden City, N.Y.: Doubleday Anchor, 1967), esp. 114–20.

15. See Dreyfus and Rubin, "You Can't Get Something For Nothing," 34–46, and the citations to Kierkegaard there.

16. See, for example, Francis A. Schaeffer, *Death in the City* (Downers Grove, Ill.: Intervarsity Press, 1969), esp. chap. 7.

6. GOD

1. This restriction, of course, is more formidable than it appears.

2. My argument has ancestors at least as far back as Pascal. The present formulation was suggested by Leszek Kolakowski, *Religion* (New York: Oxford University Press, 1982), esp. pp. 82–90, 188–97, where he discusses the maxim "If God does not exist, then everything is permitted." But Kolakowski reaches an agnostic conclusion.

3. If there is a God, the supposition of a world without Him is an absurdity. But we can still explore the implications of a possibly absurd hypothesis, as is done in the construction of arguments by *reductio ad absurdum*. (I owe this point to Robert M. Adams in conversation.)

4. Geach, *Providence and Evil* (Cambridge: Cambridge University Press, 1977), 81.

5. This sentence is directed against R. M. Hare, *Critical Thinking* (Oxford: Oxford University Press, 1981).

6. Natalya Sedova, *Vie et Mort de Leon Trotsky,* quoted in Isaac Deutscher, *The Prophet Outcast* (London: Oxford University Press, 1963), 503.

7. See Hans Reiss, ed., H. B. Nisbet, trans., *Kant's Political Writings* (Cambridge: Cambridge University Press, 1970), esp. "Idea of a Universal History with a Cosmopolitan Purpose," 41–53.

8. Compare the dispute over "evidentialism" in theology; for example, several of the articles in Robert Audi and William Wainwright, eds., *Rationality, Religious Belief, and Moral Commitment* (Ithaca, N.Y.: Cornell University Press, 1986).

9. An atheist might argue that the *via negativa* shows that the concept of God is incoherent. But such an argument requires the assumption that mysteries are excluded by universally binding rationality norms.

10. I discuss these issues in my article "The Religious Significance

of the Ontological Argument," *Religious Studies* 11 (1975): 97–116. But this article now seems to me seriously deficient.

11. At this point the problem of evil arises. I assume dogmatically that it makes sense for a state of affairs to be bad in itself and yet contribute to a universe that, as a whole, is as its morally perfect Creator wants it to be.

12. *Summa Theologiae*, Ia, Q. 44, a. 1.

13. Lewis, *Christian Reflections*, ed. Walter Hooper (Grand Rapids, Mich.: Eerdmans, 1967), 80.

14. I am here indebted to Gary Gutting.

15. *Anselmian Explorations* (Notre Dame, Ind.: University of Notre Dame Press, 1987), chap. 9.

16. See my article "The Logic of Fiction," *Philosophical Studies* 26 (December 1974), 389–99.

17. At any rate I fail to understand Morris's attempts to evade this conclusion.

18. I am indebted to Father Owen Carroll for help with this point.

19. To understand the reasons theists may have for discomfort with Neoplatonism, consider the doctrines of the late Neoplatonist Damascius, as summarized in Kolakowski, *Metaphysical Horror* (Oxford: Basil Blackwell, 1988), 43–49.

20. For a selection of perspectives on these assumptions, see the articles by Christopher Menzel, Del Ratzsch, Alvin Plantinga, and Richard Otte collected in Alvin Plantinga, ed., "Philosophy from a Christian Perspective," *Faith and Philosophy* 4 (1987), 365–447.

7. RELIGION

1. The concept of a persuasive definition was introduced by C. L. Stevenson; see his *Ethics and Language* (New Haven: Yale University Press, 1965), chap. 3. Stevenson denies, not very convincingly, that his account is intended as derogatory.

2. On the importance of evaluatively charged expressions, as well as their logic, see Julius Kovesi, *Moral Notions* (New York: Humanities Press, 1969).

3. I do not enter here the controversy over real definitions. Whether or not things can be defined, terms certainly can be.

4. Stevenson, *Ethics and Language*, 282–90. On re-emphatic definitions see ibid., 290–94.

5. The issues are spotlighted in James Hitchcock, "Church, State, and Moral Values," *Law and Contemporary Problems* 44 (Spring 1981), 3–21, and the other articles in the same issue. The most important judicial decision is *United States v. Seeger*, 380 U.S. 163 (1965); see also the thoughtful concurring opinion by Circuit Judge Adams in *Malnak v. Yogi*, 502 F 2d 197, 200–15 (1979).

6. For an example of a family-resemblance analysis of "religion," see W. P. Alston, "Religion," in *Encyclopedia of Philosophy*, ed. Paul Edwards (New York: Macmillan, 1967), vol. 7, 140–45.

7. Wilfred Cantwell Smith, *The Meaning and End of Religion* (New York: Macmillan, 1963), esp. chap. 5.

8. *Tractatus Logico-Philosophicus*, trans. D. F. Pears and B. F. McGuinness (London: Routledge and Kegan Paul, 1963), 3.

9. Kierkegaard, or at least Johannes Climacus, is quite explicit in his insistence that Christianity, which paradoxically claims that God has existed as a historical individual, is not a doctrine but an indirect communication expressing an aspect of the human situation not otherwise communicable. *Concluding Unscientific Postscript*, trans. David F. Swenson, ed. Walter Lowrie (Princeton: Princeton University Press, 1968), 290–91, 339. Readers who fail to see this point make Kierkegaard seem much more of an irrationalist than he in fact is.

10. For a more rationalistic reading of the doctrine of the Incarnation than the ones here considered, see Thomas V. Morris, *The Logic of God Incarnate* (Ithaca, N.Y.: Cornell University Press, 1986). I leave to theologians the question of whether Morris's account (or mine) is adequate to what Christians have wanted to say about Christ.

11. See Humphrey Palmer, *Analogy* (London: Macmillan, 1973), esp. chap. 13.

12. Some are; for example, R. C. Sproul, "Biblical Interpretation and the Analogy of Faith," in *Inerrancy and Common Sense*, ed. Roger R. Nicole and J. Ramsey Michaels (Grand Rapids, Mich.: Baker, 1980), chap. 5. Others are not; for example, J. Ramsey Michaels "Inerrancy or Verbal Inspiration?" and John Jefferson Davis, "Genesis, Inerrancy, and the Antiquity of Man," ibid., chaps. 2, 6. An intermediate position is J. I. Packer, *"Fundamentalism" and the Word of God* (Grand Rapids, Mich.: Eerdmans, 1972), 99, 104–6.

13. A possible example is Leszek Kolakowski, *The Key to Heaven and Conversations with the Devil*, trans. Celina Wieniewska and Salvator Attanasio (New York: Grove Press, 1972).

14. Collect, Second Sunday in Lent.

15. I discuss some problem cases for the concept of religion in my article "On the Definition of 'Religion,'" *Faith and Philosophy* 3 (1986), 275–82.

16. From now on I use Christian examples only. A superficial discussion of other traditions would be worthless, and an in-depth discussion would carry us too far afield. But I do not intend implications of this section to be limited to Christianity.

17. Two related cases should be distinguished. That Jesus was conceived by the Holy Spirit probably entails that he lacked a human father, though its implications are far larger than this. The Resurrection of Jesus entails at least the following two historical propositions: that his dead body inexplicably disappeared, and that his disciples (including St. Paul) had what they took to be appearances of their Risen Lord. It does not, I think, entail that the Risen Body of Jesus could be photographed.

18. I do not wish wholly to condemn such practices as praying in tongues. But the "words" of such prayers must somehow be connected with ordinary speech. This would also appear to be the normative Christian position; see 1 Corinthians 14.

19. Both of these principles are to be found in Pascal: "God has set up in the Church visible signs to make Himself known to those who should seek Him sincerely" (*Pensees*, trans. William F. Trotter, ed. H. S. Thayer [New York: Washington Square Press, 1965], no. 194); "God being thus hidden, every religion which does not affirm that God is hidden, is not true"(ibid., no. 585). In both of these passages Pascal is arguing, on grounds of natural reason, for the plausibility of the Christian revelation as he understands it.

20. I make no attempt to assess the theology of Calvin, for example. An adequate interpretation of a religious writer requires a sort of investigation that is out of place here.

21. At least I have been unable to find any argument that absolutely excludes the possible infallibility of religious teachers.